Perpetual Euphoria

On the Duty to Be Happy

PRINCETON UNIVERSITY PRESS

Princeton and Oxford

Originally published in French as *L'Euphorie perpétuelle: Essai sur le devoir de bonheur*, by Grasset & Fasquelle, 61, rue de Saints Peres, 75006 Paris

Copyright © 2000 by Grasset & Fasquelle

The English translation is copyright © 2010 by Princeton University Press

Published by Princeton University Press, 41 William Street,
Princeton, New Jersey 08540

In the United Kingdom: Princeton University Press, 6 Oxford Street,
Woodstock, Oxfordshire OX20 1TW

press.princeton.edu

Library of Congress Cataloging-in-Publication Data
Bruckner, Pascal.
    [Euphorie perpétuelle. English]
    Perpetual euphoria : on the duty to be happy / Pascal Bruckner;
translated by Steven Rendall.
        p.   cm.
    Includes index.
    ISBN 978-0-691-14373-6 (hardcover : alk. paper)   1. Happiness—
History—19th century.   2. Happiness—History—20th century.
3. Happiness—Social aspects.   I. Title.
    BJ1482.B7813 2010
    170—dc22

                                            2009039254

British Library Cataloging-in-Publication Data is available

Ouvrage publié avec le soutien du Centre national du livre–ministère français chargé de la culture / This work is published with support from the French Ministry of Culture/Centre national du livre

This book has been composed in Minion
Printed on acid-free paper. ∞
Printed in the United States of America
10 9 8 7 6 5 4 3 2

PERPETUAL EUPHORIA

PASCAL BRUCKNER

Translated by STEVEN RENDALL

To my mother

There are people assailed by happiness

as if it were a misfortune, and it is.

—FRANÇOIS MAURIAC

CONTENTS

INTRODUCTION
Invisible Penitence 1

PART I ❖
Paradise Is Where I Am 7

    ONE
    Life as a Dream and a Lie 9

    TWO
    The Golden Age and After? 27

    THREE
    The Disciplines of Beatitude 39

PART II ❖
The Kingdom of the Lukewarm,
or The Invention of Banality 67

    FOUR
    The Bittersweet Saga of Dullness 69

    FIVE
    The Extremists of Routine 84

    SIX
    Real Life Is Not Absent 106

PART III ◆
The Bourgeoisie, or The Abjection of Well-Being   129

SEVEN
*"The Fat, Prosperous Elevation of the Average,
the Mediocre"*   131

EIGHT
What Is Happiness for Some Is Kitsch for Others   149

NINE
If Money Doesn't Make You Happy, Give It Back!   163

PART IV ◆
Unhappiness Outlawed?   181

TEN
The Crime of Suffering   183

ELEVEN
Impossible Wisdom   206

CONCLUSION
Madame Verdurin's Croissant   227

INDEX   233

PERPETUAL EUPHORIA

Invisible Penitence

In 1738 the young Mirabeau sent a letter to his friend Vauvenargues, reproaching him for living from day to day without having any plan for achieving happiness: "See here, my friend, you think all the time, you study, and nothing is beyond the scope of your ideas; and yet you never think for a moment about making a clear plan leading to what should be our only goal: happiness." He went on to list for his skeptical correspondent the principles that guided his own conduct: ridding himself of prejudices, preferring gaiety to moodiness, following his inclinations and at the same time purifying them.[1] We may laugh at this juvenile enthusiasm. Mirabeau, who was the child of a time that thought it could reinvent the human being and do away with the plagues of the Old Regime, was concerned about his happiness the way people before him had been concerned about the salvation of their souls.

Have we changed that much? Consider today's Mirabeaus—young people of all backgrounds and opinions, anxious to begin a new era and move beyond the ruins of the frightening twentieth century. They launch out into

---

[1] Quoted in Robert Mauzi, *L'Idée de bonheur dans la littérature et la pensée française au XVIIIe siècle* (Paris: Albin Michel, 1965; rpt. Geneva: Slatkine, 1979), pp. 261–262.

life eager to exercise their rights and first of all to construct their lives as they see fit, sure that each of them has been promised everything. From their infancy they have been told: *Be happy*, because nowadays we no longer have children in order to transmit to them values or a spiritual heritage but rather to increase the number of fully realized individuals on Earth.

Be happy! Beneath this apparently amiable injunction, is there another, more paradoxical, more terrible? The commandment is all the more difficult to elude because it corresponds to no object. How can we know whether we are happy? Who sets the norm? Why do we have to be happy, why does this recommendation take the form of an imperative? And what shall we reply to those who pathetically confess: "I can't"?

In short, for our young people, this privilege quickly comes a burden: seeing themselves as solely responsible for their dreams and their successes, they find that the happiness they desire so much recedes before them as they pursue it. Like everybody else, they dream of a wonderful synthesis that combines professional, romantic, moral, and family success, and beyond each of these, like a reward, perfect satisfaction. As if the self-liberation promised by modernity were supposed to be crowned by happiness, as the diadem placed atop the whole process. But this synthesis is deferred as they elaborate it, and they experience the promise of enchantment not as a blessing but as a debt owed a faceless divinity whom they will never be able to repay. The countless miracles they were supposed to receive will trickle in randomly, embittering the quest and increasing the burden.

They are angry with themselves for not meeting the established standard, for infringing the rule. Mirabeau could still dream, conceive unrealistic projects. Three centuries later, the rather lofty ideal of an Enlightenment aristocrat has been transformed into penitence. We now have every right except the right not to be blissful.

❖ There is nothing more vague than the idea of happiness, that old prostituted, adulterated word so full of poison that we would like to exclude it from the language. Since antiquity, it has been nothing but the history of its contradictory and successive meanings: in his time, St. Augustine already counted no less than 289 differing opinions on the subject, the eighteenth century devoted almost 50 treatises to it, and we are constantly projecting onto earlier periods or other cultures a conception and obsession that belongs solely to our own. It is in the nature of this notion to be an enigma, a permanent source of debates, a fluid that can take every form, but which no form exhausts. There is a happiness of action and another of contemplation, a happiness of the mind and another of the senses, a happiness of prosperity and another of deprivation, a happiness of virtue and another of crime. Theories of happiness, Diderot said, are always only the histories of those who formulate them. Here, we are interested in a different kind of history: that of the desire to be happy as a passion peculiar to the West since the French and American revolutions.

The project of being happy encounters three paradoxes. Its object is so vague that it becomes intimidating because of its imprecision. It leads to boredom or apathy as soon it is realized (in this sense, the ideal happiness would be one that was always satisfied and always arising anew, thus avoiding the double trap of frustration and satiety). Finally, it avoids suffering to the point of being helpless when it occurs.

In the first case, the very abstraction of happiness explains its seductive power and the anguish it produces. Not only are we wary of prefabricated paradises, but we are never sure that we are truly happy. When we wonder whether we are happy, we are already no longer happy. Hence the infatuation with this state is also connected with two attitudes, conformism and envy, the conjoint ailments of democratic culture: a focus on the pleasures sought by the majority and attraction to the elect whom fortune seems to have favored.

In the second case, the concern about happiness in its secular form is contemporary in Europe with the advent of banality, a new temporal system that was set up at the dawn of the modern age and that sees secular life, reduced to its prosaic form, triumphing after the withdrawal of God. Banality or the victory of the bourgeois order: mediocrity, platitude, vulgarity.

Finally, seeking to eliminate pain nonetheless puts it at the heart of the system. As a result, today we suffer from not wanting to suffer just as one can make oneself ill by trying to be perfectly healthy. Furthermore, we now tell ourselves a strange fable about a society completely devoted to hedonism, and for which everything becomes an irritation, a torture. Unhappiness is not only unhappiness; it is, worse yet, a failure to be happy.

❖ By the duty to be happy, I thus refer to the ideology peculiar to the second half of the twentieth century that urges us to evaluate everything in terms of pleasure and displeasure, a summons to a euphoria that makes those who do not respond to it ashamed or uneasy. A dual postulate: on the one hand, we have to make the most of our lives; on the other, we have to be sorry and punish ourselves if we don't succeed in doing so. This is a perversion of a very beautiful idea: that everyone has a right to control his own destiny and to improve his life. How did a liberating principle of the Enlightenment, the right to happiness, get transformed into a dogma, a collective catechism? That is the process we will try to trace here.

The supreme Good is defined in so many different ways that we end up attaching it to a few collective ideals—health, the body, wealth, comfort, well-being—talismans upon which it is supposed to land like a bird upon bait. Means become ends and reveal their insufficiency as soon as the delight sought fails to materialize. So that by a cruel mistake, we often move farther away from happiness by the same means that were supposed to allow us to approach it. Whence the frequent mistakes made with regard to happiness: thinking that we have to demand it as our due, learn it like a subject in school, construct it the way we would a house; that it can be bought, converted into monetary terms, and finally that others procure it from a reliable source and that all we have to do is imitate them in order to be bathed in the same aura.

Contrary to a commonplace that has been tirelessly repeated ever since Aristotle (although in his work the term had a different meaning), it is not true that everyone seeks happiness, which is a Western idea that appeared at a certain point in history. There are other ideas—freedom, justice, love, friendship—that can take precedence over happiness. How can we say what all people have sought since the dawn of time without slipping into hollow generalities? I am opposing not happiness but the transformation of this fragile feeling into a veritable collective drug to which everybody is supposed to become addicted in chemical, spiritual, psychological, digital, and religious forms. The most elaborate wisdom and sciences have to confess their inability to guarantee the felicity of peoples and individuals. Felicity, every time it touches us, produces a feeling of having received a grace, a favor, not that of a calculation, a specific mode of behavior. And perhaps we experience the good things of the world, opportunities, pleasures, and good fortune to the degree that we have abandoned the dream of attaining Beatitude with a capital letter.

To the young Mirabeau, we would like to reply: "I love life too much to want to be merely happy!"

PART I

Paradise Is Where I Am

CHAPTER ONE

Life as a Dream and a Lie

This world is only a bridge. Cross it,
but don't build your house on it.

—Henn. Apocrypha, 35

Blessed are those who mourn,
for they shall be comforted.

—Beatitudes (Matthew 5:4)

"A Christian Is a Man of the Other World" (Bossuet)

In sixteenth-century France and Italy, there were collective
autos-da-fé or "bonfires of the vanities," in which, as a sign
of their renunciation of the trifles of the world, men and
women threw into the flames playing cards, books, jewels,
wigs, and perfumes.[1] During this period at the end of the
Middle Ages, which was tormented by a strong passion for
life, doubt was not permitted: full satisfaction was to be had
only in God, and everything outside God was mere trick-
ery and dissimulation. Thus it was necessary constantly to

---

[1] Johan Huizinga, *The Autumn of the Middle Ages*, trans. Rodney J. Payton
and Ulrich Mammitzsch (Chicago: University of Chicago Press, 1996), p. 7.

remind mortals of the insignificance of human pleasures in comparison with those awaiting them in Paradise.

Contrary to Saint-Just's famous aphorism, happiness has never been a new idea in Europe, and from the outset Christianity, loyal to its Greek heritage, recognized the aspiration to happiness. But it put happiness beyond man's reach, in Eden or in heaven (the eighteenth century limited itself to bringing it into the secular world). We all recall having been happy before the Fall, St. Augustine said; and there is no happiness except in reminiscence, since in the depths of memory it is the living spring of God that we rediscover. Writing about our futile means of gaining access to the supreme good, Pascal wrote: "What is it that arouses in us this avidity and impotence if it is not that there was once in man a genuine happiness of which only the mark and the empty trace now remain to us?"

This Christian temporal trinity was later adopted by both religious and agnostic authors: happiness existed yesterday or will exist tomorrow, in nostalgia or in hope, but it never exists today. Although it is legitimate to tend toward that condition, it would be madness to try to accomplish it in this world. As a fallen creature, man must first redeem the sin of existing, he must work on his salvation. And salvation is all the more anguishing because it is gained or lost once and for all, as Georges Dumézil pointed out: for the Christian, there are no second chances, in contrast to Hindus and Buddhists, who are caught up in the cycle of reincarnations until they finally gain deliverance. It is during my brief residence on Earth that my eternal fate is decided, and this perspective gives the temporal accident I represent the appearance of a genuine challenge. It is typical of Christianity to have overdramatized our existence by subjecting it to the alternative between hell and paradise. The life of the believer is a trial that takes place entirely before the divine Judge. "All the evil done by the wicked is recorded, and they do not know it," says the psalmist. Our sins and our merits are inscribed one by one in the great account book, with a credit or a debit balance. Even if sinners, unfaithful women and corrupt men, "take cover in all the darkness of the night, they shall be discovered and judged" (Bossuet). A terrible disproportion: a tiny human error can lead to eternal punishment, but inversely, all our sufferings can find their reward in the beyond if we have led lives pleasing to God. Pass or fail: paradise is structured like a school.

The itinerary of salvation, although it postulates a relative freedom for the believer, who can perfect himself or succumb to worldly passions, is far from straight. It moves in a world of chiaroscuro, and the sincerest of the faithful see their faith as a pilgrimage into a labyrinth. Because He is both very close and infinitely distant, the path to God is full of ambushes and pitfalls. "God is properly known only when he is known as an unknown," said St. Thomas. Thus we have to sojourn in this world in accord with the laws of another, and the world that dazzles us with its countless enchantments is both the enemy and the ally of salvation. That is why although this life cannot usurp the dignity that belongs to God alone, it nonetheless has a sacred character; we have to pass through it because it is the first step toward eternal life. For a Christian, time is not a guarantee of the beyond but a tension filled with fears, doubts, and heartbreaks. The hope of redemption is thus inseparable from a fundamental worry. "We understand nothing of God's works if we do not take as our principle that he wanted to blind some and enlighten others. . . . There is always enough darkness to blind the outcast and enough light to condemn them and make them inexcusable" (Pascal). And when Luther substitutes salvation through works for salvation through faith—God alone makes the sovereign decision whether we will be saved or damned, whatever we do or wish—he maintains a certain degree of uncertainty in the elect. The latter are never sure that they have been chosen, even if they show their fervor through pious acts. Whatever the sinner's behavior, he can never redeem his debt to God; he can only count on God's infinite mercy. In other words, salvation is a narrow gate whereas the way that leads to perdition is "wide and easy"[2] (Matthew 7:13).

Given this terrible requirement of either gaining eternity or sinking into sin, what importance can the little happinesses of life have? None! They are not only ephemeral and deceptive—"The world, poor in results, is always magnificent in promises" (Bossuet)—but also draw us away from the true path, throw us into a lamentable enslavement to earthly goods. "All opulence that does not come from my God is poverty to me," St. Augustine splendidly wrote. A double anathema is cast upon pleasures: they are ridiculous in comparison to the beatitude that awaits us in

[2] Quoted by John-Paul II, *Le Sens Chrétien de la souffrance* (Paris: Pierre Tequi, 1984), p. 68.

heaven and are mere reflections of a permanence and so-
lidity that belong to the divine order alone. They represent
the bad infinity of concupiscence, which is an inverted image of celestial bliss. In this case, mortals' error is to take
nonbeing for being. Worldly joys are pulverized in the
terrible perspective of death, whose shadow, Bossuet tells
us, "darkens everything."[3] It is death that makes health a
mere reprieve, glory a chimera, pleasures an infamy, and
life a dream combined with a lie. Death does not come
from afar but is right next to us, it insinuates itself into the
very air we breathe, into the food we eat, into the remedies
with which we try to protect ourselves. Pascal comments:
"Death, which threatens us at every moment, must before
long inevitably confront us with the terrible necessity of
being either annihilated or unhappy." To disqualify all of
our existence in light of the tomb is to emphasize that from
the day of our birth we are plunged into a torpor to which
our death agony puts an end. Life is a slumber from which
we must awaken: this metaphor, borrowed from Antiquity
and omnipresent in Christian thought, makes death a fatal
moment in every sense of the term. There are, in a sense,
three deaths: physical death; death in life for those who live
in a state of sin, that is, in disunion with God, in spiritual
mourning (in some Breton churches hell is represented as a
cold, icy place of separation); and finally, for the righteous,
death as liberation and transition. In the latter case, death
is not an abyss but a gateway leading to the Kingdom of
God, and it makes the soul "capable of enjoying an infinity

[3] Jacques-Bénigne Bossuet, *Sermons et oraisons funèbres* (Paris: Seuil), pp.
140–141.

of satisfactions not to be found in this life."[4] It is absurd to fear annihilation because by freeing us from the body and its turmoil, death constitutes the beginning of an unprecedented adventure, that of the Last Judgment and eternal Resurrection.

This, then, is the Christian calculus: it opposes to the very natural fear of suffering and death the still greater fear of perdition. And it promises that the wretched of this world will be rewarded in the next, the only way to put an end to the scandal of the prosperity of the wicked and the misery of the righteous. It urges us to put our faith in an immaterial good or evil—paradise or hell—so as to throw a chaste veil over the very real ordeals we face today. To renounce the false prestige of this world is to have a right to an enormous reward in heaven. This is a subtle calculus that clothes resignation in a luminous garment: since "no one can serve two masters . . . God and Mammon" (Matthew 6:24), I abandon concrete, immediate joys for a hypothetical future pleasure. Why should we cling to a few instants of joy on Earth at the risk of frying forever in Satan's realm? The major crime, on which all churchmen insist, is not being tempted by earthly fruits but being attached to them, being so enslaved to them that we forget the fundamental bond with God. If we don't want to fail this test, it is "the matter of eternity to which all our efforts must be directed" (Bossuet), because "the only good thing in this life is the hope of another" (Pascal). In any case, the pathos of salvation must win out over the desire for happiness.

[4] René Descartes, *Correspondance avec la princesse Palatine sur "La Vie heureuse" de Sénèque* (Paris: Arlea, 1989), pp. 188–189.

Fortunately, this process has not always been put under the sign of an inflexible "either/or." It is the function of the sacraments, and in particular that of penitence, to relieve the man of faith from a terrible tension and allow him to alternate sin with repentance and absolution in an oscillation that scandalized Calvin and Freud as well.[5] Above all, in the eleventh century the Catholic Church had the brilliant idea of inventing, under popular pressure and in response to millenarianism, the notion of purgatory, an enormous waiting room, a third position located between heaven and hell that allowed those whose lives had been mediocre, neither completely good nor completely bad, to erase their debt to God. This posthumous make-up class also gave the living a way of acting on the dead and communicating with them through their prayers. Purgatory not only alleviated the Church's terrible blackmail of the faithful that consisted in subjecting them to a choice between freedom and damnation (we have to remember that hell, in its terrifying, incandescent version, was an invention of the Renaissance and not the Middle Ages[6]). It also set up a whole system for "mitigating punishment,"[7] thus introducing into religion the notion of negotiation, which led to all the excesses we know about and provoked the ire of reformers scandalized to see Rome selling indulgences,

---

[5] In his preface to the *Brothers Karamazov*, Freud, discussing the moralist in Dostoyevsky who uses and abuses repentance, writes: "He makes us think of the barbarians of the invasions who killed and then did penance; as a result, penance became a technique that permitted murder."

[6] As Jean Delumeau reminds us in his book *La Peur en Occident* (Paris: Fayard, 1978), chap. 7, on Satanism.

[7] Jacques Le Goff, *La Naissance du Purgatoire* (Paris: Gallimard, 1981).

that is, to see a human institution issuing drafts on eternity and thus, as it were, forcing God's hand.[8] Thanks to purgatory, life on Earth becomes sweeter, more lovable. The idea of the irreversible fades; a sin limited in time ceases to entail an infinite loss. By changing the "geography of the beyond," purgatory leaves a door open on the future and avoids discouragement, it "cools down" human history. As a result of this tranquilizing psychology, the sinner no longer feels hellfire licking at his heels as soon as he does something that is forbidden. Expiation remains possible, and salvation loses the inhumanity given it by dogma. The Reformation itself, despite its doctrinal intransigence, had the paradoxical effect of rehabilitating life on Earth by its effort to incarnate the values of the other world in the here and now. Luther demanded that people foreswear idleness and act in order to please God, arguing that "a good,

[8] As early as the twelfth century, the system of setting a price on penance spread in France and took the form of gifts of money, prayers, or masses. The latter were sold by the unit, as preparation for the beyond. With the development of religiousness connected with indulgences, the most unbridled mercantile transactions flourished: by making pilgrimages, giving to charitable orders, or reciting psalms, people hoped to reduce the number of years they would have to endure in purgatory. "For example, one sanctuary might promise, in return for confessions, gifts, and prayers, to acquire seven years and seven quarantines [periods of forty days], while another might promise to acquire forty times forty years. A pilgrim's guide to the Holy Land tells us that a systematic tour of the holy places will bring in, so to speak, forty-three times seven years and seven quarantines." Quoted in Jacques Chiffoleau, "Crise de la croyance," *Histoire de la France religieuse* (Paris: Seuil, 1988), vol. 2, pp. 138, 142. Let us recall that to the great indignation of Protestants, the Catholic church continues to grant indulgences, though it does not charge for them. The papal bull issued in 2000 accords penitents who have abstained from drinking and smoking for one year full indulgences that can be applied to the dead in purgatory.

righteous man does good works"[9] and thus confirms his chances of being saved.

In the same way, in the seventeenth century there developed an accommodating Christianity that did not want to choose heaven over Earth, but rather to couple the two. Far from being incompatible, one follows the other, and Malebranche, rejecting the terms of Pascal's wager, showed that happiness was an ascent from worldly pleasures to celestial joys, in which the soul moves steadily toward final illumination. Whereas others emphasized a rupture, he reestablished a continuity and in a very modern view of religion described man as driven by the same impulse toward eternity and the quest for temporal goods. Now nature and grace collaborate harmoniously in shaping human destinies: a Christian can be a gentleman, combining politeness with piety,"[10] and busy himself with everyday tasks without losing sight of the perspective of redemption. Immortality is democratized; it becomes accessible to the multitude. Thus Christianity remains the doctrine of a relative and reasoned devaluation of the world: by considering this life as the site of perdition and salvation, it makes it both an obstacle to and a condition for deliverance and thereby raises it to the status of the sovereign good; it frees us from the body but restores the latter's rights through the doctrine of incarnation. In short, it affirms human autonomy even as it subordinates it to divine transcendence. In both cases, it asks the believer, who is caught between "the

---

[9] In *Les Grands Écrits réformateurs* (Paris: Garnier-Flammarion), p. 222.

[10] Quoted in Mauzi, *L'Idée de bonheur dans la littérature et la pensée française au XVIIIe siècle*, pp. 17, 18, 181.

perils of enjoyment" and the rejection of "the enchanting and dangerous sweetness of life" (St. Augustine), to accept the world of the senses without idolizing it, without raising mundane things to the rank of absolutes.

On the Formula "How's It Going?"

"How's it going?" People have not always greeted each other in this way: they invoked divine protection for themselves, and they did not bow before a commoner the way they bowed before a nobleman. In order for the formula "How's it going?" to appear, we had to leave the feudal world and enter the democratic era, which presupposes a minimal degree of equality between individuals, subject to oscillations in their moods. According to one legend, the French expression "ça va?" is of medical origin: how do you defecate? A vestige of a time when intestinal regularity was seen as a sign of good health.

This lapidary, standardized formality corresponds to the principle of economy and constitutes the minimal social bond in a mass society that seeks to include people from all over. But it is sometimes less a routine than a way of intimating something: we want to force the person met to situate himself, we want to petrify him, subject him to a detailed examination. What are you up to? What's happened to you? A discreet summons that commands everyone to expose himself for what he really is. In a world that makes movement a canonical value, there is an interest in how things are going, even if we don't know where. That's why a "how's it going?" that expects no answer is more human than one that is full of concern but wants to strip you bare and force you to give a moral accounting for yourself. This is because the fact of being is no longer taken for granted, and we have to pay permanent attention to our internal barometers. Are things going as well as I say, or am I embellishing them? That is why many people evade the question and move to another topic, assuming that the interlocutor is perceptive enough to discern in their "fine" a discreet depression. Then there is this terrible expression of renunciation: "Okay, I guess," as if one had to let the days and hours pass without taking part in them. But why, after all, do things have to be going well? Asked daily to justify ourselves, it often happens that we are so opaque to ourselves that the answer no longer has any meaning other than as a formality.

"You're looking good today." Flowing over us like honey, this compliment has the effect of a kind of consecration: in the confrontation between the radiant and the grouchy, I am on the right side. And now I am, through a bit of verbal magic, raised to the summit of a subtle and ever-changing hierarchy. But the following day another, ruthless verdict is handed down: "You look terrible today." This observation executes me at point-blank range, deprives me of the splendid position where I thought I had taken up permanent residence. I have not proven worthy of the caste of the magnificent, I am a pariah and have to slink along walls, trying to conceal the fact that I look ill.

Ultimately, "how's it going?" is the most futile and the most profound of questions. To answer it precisely, one would have to make a scrupulous inventory of one's psyche, considering each aspect in detail. No matter: we have to say "fine" out of politeness and civility and change the subject, or else ruminate the question during our whole lives and reserve our reply for afterward.

Beloved Suffering

For Christianity, what is unhappiness? The price we pay for
the Fall, the liability we have accrued as a result of original
sin. In this regard, the churches have overdone it: not only
do they castigate this world, but they make life a matter
of atoning for a sin that stains us all from birth because
it has contaminated the countless descendants of Adam
and Eve. We are all guilty, even the fetus in its mother's
belly; whence the urgency of baptizing the newborn. But
it would be irresponsible to make this wretchedness connected with our imperfection a cause for despair. It was out
of love that the Lord gave his only begotten son to deliver
humanity from evil. The fact that the emblem of this religion is a crucified man on his cross means that it has put
the death of God at the heart of its ritual. By dying, Jesus
becomes "death's owner" (Paul Valéry) and converts death
into joy. Mourning and resurrection: the son of God on his
cross affirms the tragic nature of the human condition and
transcends it in the direction of the superhuman order of
hope and love. Jesus's passion thus allows every unhappy
person to relive it at his own level and to participate in a
founding event that is greater than he is. Even degraded, he
has to carry his own cross and find in Jesus a guide and a
friend who will help him. On the condition that his suffering becomes not a mortal enemy but an ally endowed with
a power to purify and provide a "renewal of spiritual energy" (John Paul II). It has, as the philosopher Max Scheler
put it, a unique capacity to separate the authentic from the
futile, the inferior from the superior, to free man from the

confusion of the senses, from the crude dross of the body, and direct his gaze toward the essential riches.[11]

Thus it is not enough to undergo suffering, one has to love it, make it a lever to produce a real transformation. It is the defeat that leads to victory and, as Luther said, it is by damning the sinner that God assures his salvation. "Every man becomes the church's path, especially when suffering comes into his life."[12] In this way Christianity rejects both aristocratic heroism and the Stoic ethics that commands us to accept losses and illnesses without complaining, and even asks the wise man to undergo torture with a smile. Pascal blasted Epictetus's pride in facing misfortune, which he saw as an insolent assertion of a human freedom unaware of its impotence. It is impossible to escape suffering the way the ancients did, to elude it by all sorts of stratagems or to exclaim sacrilegiously, like the Epicureans, "Death does not exist for us." One has to acknowledge one's ordeal, cry out in one's ignominy, and from the depths of this degradation rise up to God. "Suffering saves existence," Simone Weil wrote, "it is never strong enough, never great enough." Because it opens the doors to knowledge and wisdom, "the more unjust it is, the better."[13]

Whence the inevitable attraction to pain in Protestant, Orthodox, and Catholic Christianity, a very real concern for the suffering that is accompanied by an attraction to unhappiness. "Christ taught us to do good by suffering

[11] Max Scheler, *Le Sens de la souffrance* (Paris: Aubier, 1921), pp. 65ff.
[12] John Paul II, *Le Sens Chrétien de la souffrance*, p. 4.
[13] Simone Weil, *La Pesanteur et la grâce* (1948; rpt. Paris: Plon, 1988).

and to do good to those who suffer."[14] This explains the compulsive need to seize upon the suffering of others, as if one's own were not enough (thus the Polish clergy's attempt to transform Auschwitz into a modern Golgotha, or the solicitation for souls in which, according to some journalists, Mother Teresa engaged in her hospices in Calcutta, however great her merits may be in other respects). Or again the pronounced taste for martyrdom, dismembered bodies, and the obsession with carrion and decay in a certain kind of Christian art, the accent being put on the body's excremental nature, and finally the aesthetics of torture and blood in the mystics. Few religions have emphasized human filth as much as this one or shown such a "sadism of piety."[15]

Even if since Pius XII the Church has shown itself to be more understanding with regard to sufferers, for Catholicism *it is suffering that constitutes the norm, whereas health is a quasi-anomaly.* Consider this reflection by John Paul II: "When the body is seriously ill and reduced to helplessness, when the human person finds it almost impossible to live and act, internal maturity and spiritual grandeur become all the more evident and provide a moving lesson for those who enjoy a normal state of health."[16] We have to love humans, but first they have to be humiliated, degraded. Suffering, by bringing us closer to God, is an opportunity to make progress; it loses what is worst in it: arbitrariness. John Paul II goes on: "To Job's question:

[14] John Paul II, *Le Sens Chrétien de la souffrance*, p. 91.
[15] Chiffoleau, "Crise de la croyance," p. 135.
[16] Jean Paul II, *Le Sens Chrétien de la souffrance*, p. 73.

Why is there suffering? Why me? I obtain a response only by suffering along with Christ, by accepting the call that he sends me from the height of his Cross: Follow me."[17] Only then can I find inner peace and spiritual joy in my misery. The Christian world may seem cruel to us, but it is a world saturated with meaning (like Buddhism, which makes pain the result of sins committed in earlier lives— to use the conventional formula, these sins are arrows that we have shot and that have turned back against us. A barbarous conception but an eminently consoling one). With religion, suffering becomes a mystery that we can decipher only by suffering. A strange mystery, moreover, that explains everything.[18] And theologians developed treasures of casuistry and subtlety to justify the existence of evil without denying that God is all good.

We now see the importance of dying ostentatiously in the early modern period (and down to the middle of the twentieth century in rural areas). It used to be taken for granted, when people lived in a common habitat, that a person's death could take place only in public, witnessed by others, and not alone in a hospital, as is now the case. In the ultimate test, the believer found an opportunity to settle his accounts with those near to him, to meditate on his sins, and to free himself from terrestrial bonds before embarking upon the invisible. "It is not shameful for a

[17] Ibid., p. 76.
[18] In his *Orientation philosophique* (Paris: PUF, 1990), p. 56, Marcel Conche explains that "by a curious mechanism, thanks to the absence of an answer, we have an answer to everything." The notion of mystery used indiscriminately becomes a mere sophism to justify the unjustifiable, in this case, the suffering of children.

man to die in pain," said Pascal, "it is shameful to die in pleasure." The death agony is of capital importance: it allows the believer to leave his body, enduring pain, a little like a ship whose moorings are cut one by one. The death rattle and the death throes are supposed to testify to a life wholly oriented toward religious devotion and charity.

Thus Bossuet excoriates lukewarm believers whose faith awakens at death's threshold in the form of a tardy repentance; but he praises at length the fourteen-year-old Henriette Anne d'Angleterre, Duchess of Orléans, who, as death approached, called the priests rather than the doctors, asked for the sacraments, and cried out: "O my God, have I not always trusted in you?" Quoting St. Anthony, Bossuet continues: "The miracle of death is that for the Christian it does not end life, it ends only his sins and the dangers to which he is exposed. God cuts short not only our days but also our temptations, that is, all the risks of losing the true life, eternal life, whereas the world is nothing but our common exile."[19] So that we are not surprised to find John Paul II mentioning euthanasia and the last instants of life and praising "the person who voluntarily accepts suffering and forgoes treatment to reduce pain in order to retain all his lucidity and, if he is a believer, to take part in the Lord's Passion," even if—and the concession is important—such "heroic" behavior "cannot be considered a duty for everyone."[20] The Roman Catholic Church, as we know, accepts palliative care on the condition that it does not deprive the dying person of consciousness.

[19] Bossuet, *Sermons et oraisons funèbres*, pp. 178–179.
[20] *Evangelium Vitae* (Paris: Cerf-Flammarion, 1995), pp. 103–104.

We have to conclude that such a mechanism for justifying suffering was not very convincing because it gradually came to be regarded as a breviary of resignation and obscurantism (even by those believers who espoused secular values on this point). The discovery of pain-relieving drugs, the use of anesthetics, and the refinement of aspirin and morphine have swept away the priests' fabrications regarding pain as a necessary divine punishment. In reality, Christianity itself aroused the protest that was to weaken it. Once the notion of beatitude—even if it was located in heaven—had been posited, it unleashed a process that was ultimately to turn against it. (And the beatitudes in the Gospels, which are associated with maledictions, are not a promise of pacification but of justice. It is a call to turn the world upside down, an opportunity offered to those who are falling or have fallen: the powerful will be cast down, the wretched raised to the highest rank.[21])

Knowing what condition awaits them after death makes people impatient to experience a few glimmers of it in this world. A powerful hope for a better life emerges that draws its energy from the Scriptures themselves. People want to hasten the end of time, when the Messiah will return and the accumulation of suffering will be overthrown in a joyous Apocalypse; they count the years and centuries that separate us from that end, and the calculations inflame their minds. In this respect heretics and millenarians are

[21] "Blessed are you poor, for yours is the kingdom of God. . . . But woe to you that are rich, for you have received your consolation. . . . Woe to you that laugh now, for you shall mourn and weep," etc. Luke 6:20, 24, 25; cf. Matthew 5–7.

simply hasty readers who take the Bible's words literally and believe in their literal meaning. They emphasize Jesus's inflexibility in order to challenge the petrified forms of the ecclesiastical institution. The theme of happiness comes from Christianity, but it flourishes against it. As Hegel was the first to note, this religion contains within it everything required to transcend it and leave the domain of the religious behind. For people of the Renaissance and Enlightenment, its principal defect was to wrap suffering and misfortune in the veils of eloquence, "that eloquence of the Cross" that promises resurrection in order to distract the pious from the duty to improve their terrestrial condition. All the more so because the cult of pain and sacrifice, as Nietzsche noted with regard to the ancients, does not elevate man but rather hardens his heart and makes him bitter. Then, to adopt Karl Marx's famous formula, "to abolish religion as the illusory happiness of the people is to demand its real happiness." Catholic or Protestant severity fought desperately against human nature and its joys. With the Enlightenment, pleasure and well-being were finally rehabilitated and suffering brushed aside as an archaism. We might think history had turned a page. But on the contrary, this is where the difficulties begin.

CHAPTER TWO

The Golden Age and After?

A Marvelous Promise

In his poem *Le Mondain* (1736), Voltaire formulated the postulate on which the whole modern notion of happiness is based: "The earthly paradise is where I am," a generative matrix that people endlessly imitated or repeated, as if to convince themselves that it was true.[1] A magnificent, shocking statement that demolishes centuries of backworld and asceticism and whose disturbing simplicity we are still thinking through. Later on, Voltaire, frightened like all his contemporaries by the Lisbon earthquake, rejected this flamboyant optimism, this provocative praise of luxury and pleasure, and, confronted by the arbitrariness of nature and humans, adopted a more moderate attitude: "Someday, everything will be fine, that's what we hope. Everything is fine now—that's the illusion."[2] But for Voltaire, evil will never be

---

[1] For example, Heinrich Heine: "Bring the Kingdom down to earth." Pierre Leroux in 1849: "Paradise must come to earth." Ernst Bloch in 1921: "Now it is impossible that the time of the Kingdom is not at hand." André Breton: "Is it you, Nadja? is it true that the beyond, all the beyond, is in this life?" Paul Éluard: "There is another world but it is wholly present in this one." And Albert Camus: "My Kingdom is entirely of this world."

[2] On Voltaire's views regarding evil, see Bronislaw Bazcko's very complete study, *Job mon ami* (Paris: Gallimard, 1997), and Ernst Cassirer, *The Philosophy of the Enlightenment*, trans. F.C.A. Koelln and J. P. Pettegrove (1932) (Boston: Beacon, 1951), pp. 147–148.

invested with any positive meaning, will never be the price to be paid for sin or a consequence of the Fall, and in that respect he is a disenchanted modern. The Enlightenment and the French Revolution not only proclaimed the erasure of original sin but entered into history as a promise of happiness addressed to humanity as a whole. Happiness is no longer a metaphysical chimera, an implausible goal to be sought by means of all the complex mysteries of salvation; it is here and now, now or never.

This is a fundamental upheaval, a shift in the axis of history: Jeremy Bentham, the British father of utilitarianism, demanded the "the greatest happiness for the greatest number,"[3] Adam Smith saw in men's desire to improve their condition a sign of the divine, and John Locke recommended that we avoid uneasiness. In short, everywhere people were becoming convinced that it was reasonable to hope for the establishment of well-being on Earth. This reflected a marvelous confidence in man's perfectibility, in his ability to free himself from eternal brooding on unhappiness, and in his will to create something new—that is, something better. A confidence in the combined powers of science, education, and commerce to bring about the golden age of humanity that the utopian Saint-Simon predicted in 1814 would be realized within a few generations (thus remaining faithful to the inspiration of Francis Bacon, who in *The New Atlantis* [1626] had presented a plan for an ideal city governed by scientists). And finally, a certainty that humanity alone is responsible for the ills it inflicts on itself

---

[3] Jeremy Bentham, preface to *A Fragment on Government* (1776).

and that it alone can remedy them, correct them without recourse to a Great Clockmaker or to a church that issues rulings from the beyond. An intoxicating feeling of a messianic dawn, a new beginning of time that can transform this valley of tears into a valley of roses. History no longer fouls the air, it perfumes it, and the world once again becomes a common home whose future is as important as the concern for our personal destiny after death. In view of the fact that since the Middle Ages the gap between humanity and its Creator has never ceased to grow, man must rely solely on his own strength to organize his life on Earth. Existence as a whole must be a demonstration of good, said Dupont de Nemours, parodying Leibnizian optimism.

The hope of happiness triumphed as ideas of salvation and grandeur waned, in a double rejection of religion and feudal heroism: *We prefer to be happy rather than sublime or saved*. What had changed since the Renaissance was that following economic and technological progress, life on Earth had ceased to be seen as a penance or burden. When humans became capable of reducing misery and controlling their destiny, their self-disgust diminished. Everywhere, the decline of the "bitter taste of life" (Huizinga) that had arisen in Europe in the Middle Ages led people to see their habitat more favorably; everywhere a rehabilitation of instinct was under way, "a conquest of the pleasant" (Paul Bénichou). The world could be a fertile garden and not a sterile prison; pleasures were real and pain was no longer the sum total of human experience (as is shown by the whole utopian tradition that began with Thomas More and Campanella). Above all, people had to reconcile themselves with the body;

it was no longer the ephemeral and disgusting envelope of the soul that one had to mistrust and slough off. Now the body was a friend, our sole skiff on Earth, a loyal companion that we should support and care for, treat with all sorts of medical and hygienic procedures; whereas religion urged us to muzzle, scorn, and forget it. A triumph of comfort, the apotheosis of the padded, stuffed, and convenient, of everything that absorbed shocks and guaranteed well-being.

In short, Western societies dared to rebel against their own traditions by responding to pain *not with the consolations of the beyond but with the improvement of this world.* An act of unprecedented audacity that the American Declaration of Independence hastened to include in its articles by asserting that "life, liberty, and the pursuit of happiness" are inalienable human rights. Henceforth, humanity has to justify itself to itself alone. As Kant eloquently put it: "whether the present delivers on its promise of the future depends on us," and this promise is less prescriptive than "seductive," that is, it involves a reshaping of our planet in accord with human desires.[4] The idea of progress supplants that of eternity, and the future becomes the refuge of hope, the place where man is reconciled with himself. In him converge individual and collective felicities, particularly in Anglo-Saxon utilitarianism, which seeks to put happiness in the service of the human race as a whole in order to escape the accusations of immorality made against it. According to utilitarianism, right conduct is always associated with pleasure, and wrong conduct with pain. Thus humanity

[4] Immanuel Kant, *Théorie et pratique* (Paris: Garnier-Flammarion), pp. 34–35.

is constantly moving toward the Good, and while moral progress may sometimes "be interrupted, it is never halted" (Kant). Human time is pregnant with the seeds of happiness, and everything becomes possible, including what was previously inconceivable, and that is the conviction that underlies the aspiration to more justice and equality. We seem to have put the dreadful medieval darkness behind us forever. For the most enthusiastic, Condorcet for instance, happiness is simply inevitable, it is inherent in the triumphal advance of the human mind and is both irreversible and infallible. Alluding to the French Revolution, he wrote that "a single moment has put a century of distance between today's man and the man of tomorrow." It is impossible not to desire one's own happiness; it is a natural law of the human heart just like the laws of matter in the physical world; it is the moral counterpart of universal gravitation.

The Ambiguities of Eden

However, the promised land in the future recedes before us and strangely resembles the Christian beyond. It evaporates every time we try to seize it, disappoints us as soon as we approach it. Whence the ambiguities of the idea of progress: it is a call for effort, courage, and the hope of succeeding where earlier generations failed, but it is also a defense of present suffering in the name of an improvement postponed to an enchanting but distant future. "Tomorrow" once again becomes the eternal category of sacrifice, and historical optimism takes on the appearance of an endless purgation. Eden will always come later on. And the secular posterity of Christian pain turns out to be fertile: Hegel saw in the torments endured in the course of time necessary stages in the development of the Spirit; Marx celebrated violence as the midwife of History and advocated the ousting of the exploiting classes in order to hasten the construction of a perfect society; and in general there are all the ideologies that ask us to sacrifice the part to the whole. Such doctrines see evil as an element of the good and discern in the most terrible torments the secret labors of reason. On that basis any calamity can be justified if it has a role in the general economy of the universe, all destruction prepares the way for later reconstruction, and history is a series of errors that gradually become truths. Nightmares are dissipated: the worst horrors that people inflict on themselves necessarily contribute to the full development of all. In this respect Hegel's statement, "If by chance something could not be assimilated and dissolved in a concept, we would have to see in it the greatest scission, the greatest misfortune,"[5] holds for modernity as a whole. When distress proliferates, it invalidates all the explanations, all the sophisms, mocks the claim to identify the real with the rational. With regard to suffering, modern thinkers, in spite of themselves, are no less deluded than their religious ancestors. *That is because suffering wounds their pride by issuing a scathing denial of their omnipotence.* We know that in France, for example, it was not until the early twentieth century that physicians were obliged to relieve terminal patients' suffering (and

[5] G.W.F. Hegel, *La Raison dans l'histoire* (Paris: 10/18), p. 212.

to recognize that of newborns); up to that time, they had treated it merely as a revealing symptom. But the extraordinary quibbles used by philosophers, ideologues, and the powers that be to justify pain and misfortune collided with one ineluctable fact: democratic societies are characterized by a growing aversion to suffering. We are all the more scandalized by the latter's persistence or spread because we can no longer resort to God for consolation. In that way the Enlightenment gave rise to a certain number of contradictions from which we have still not emerged.

Christianity did not insist on its moral requirements being translated in this world in more than an embryonic way. In this world there was only imperfection and mediocrity, and the hope of redemption was deferred to the beyond. The share of ordinary creatures was cowardice and selfishness; that of the righteous and the saints was the obligation to bear witness to another order, to lavish love and charity on others. In other words, religions will always have a constitutive advantage over secular ideologies: they do not need to provide proof. The promises they make us are not on the human or temporal scale, unlike our human ideals, which have to adhere to the law of verification. That is even what killed communism, which died from the abrupt telescoping of the miracles predicted and the ignominy achieved. It is not enough to proclaim paradise on Earth, it still has to be realized in the form of improved living conditions and pleasures, at the ever-present risk of disappointing people's expectations.

This first constraint is accompanied by another. Religion discourages representations of paradise that are too exact:

this place of absolute delights, where hunger, thirst, wicked-
ness, and time do not exist, where resurrected bodies will be
endowed with eternal youth amid a radiant chorus of angels
and saints, could not be depicted too precisely. The Catholic
church, unlike millenarian sects, has always interpreted the
eschatological texts as allegories; this is religious wisdom
that holds for all monotheisms: the divine resides beyond
the range of any human imagination. Heaven consists of
a sum of delights, a "beatific vision" brought to a degree of
incandescence that we cannot even conceive. Anyone who
saw God face to face would be immediately struck down:
God is by nature invisible, nonrepresentable, inconceivable.
We cannot say what he is, only what he is not; we can speak
of him "only by negation" (Dionysius Areopagiticus).

The power of the idea of salvation consists in its being
an ineffable ecstasy in proximity to the Lord. Religious
thought has as its "strict condition that salvation must in no
case occur,"[6] whereas the requirement of the secular goal
of happiness is that it must be realized without delay. It is
the misfortune of the profane world that it cannot tolerate
vagueness and procrastination. In this respect there may be
a certain wisdom in the idea of progress, in the tacit recognition that the present instant does not exhaust all possible pleasures. The suspicion that paradise, if it were to be
brought down to Earth, might provide us with an eternity
of boredom, and the tacit desire never to see our wishes entirely realized for fear that we would be disappointed, also
explain the seductiveness of progress: it gives time a chance

---

[6] Clément Rosset, *L'Objet singulier* (Paris: Minuit, 1985), p. 17.

to ripen new pleasures while at the same time renewing old ones. Other objects of desire shimmer in the future. As a result, contrary to Hegel's famous adage, happiness can have a history. It is summed up in the way in which each period, each society, outlines its vision of the desirable and distinguishes the pleasant from the intolerable. Happiness depends on immediate enjoyment as much as it does on the hope of being able to discover new sources of joy, new perfections.

The Persistence of Pain

As soon as the goal of life is no longer to do one's duty but rather to enjoy oneself, the slightest discomfort strikes us as an affront. For the eighteenth century as well as for us today, the persistence of suffering, that inexhaustible scourge of the human race, remains an absolute obscenity. Christianity, in its great prudence, never proposed to eradicate evil on Earth: a mad ambition to which the Pelagians adhered and that was a kind of idolatry. Pascal rightly described as insane man's will to seek in himself the remedy for all his ills. The Enlightenment believed in the regeneration of the human race through the combined efforts of science, industry, and reason. This belief contained not unbridled optimism but rather a carefully proportioned mixture of calculation and benevolence: we can overcome almost all the problems that cast a shadow over us. It is just a question of time and patience. But pain, which tirelessly returns, contradicts this illusion that the world can be perfectly rationalized. Henceforth, it is up to man, without the help of Providence, to eliminate pain and suffering as far as he can, a responsibility that is as inspiring as it is crushing. There was a certain comfort in original sin, an optimism in that intimate hell in which each of us shares and which relieves the individual of a burden that overwhelms the human race as a whole. There is ultimately nothing tragic in it: the worst atrocities of history confirm original sin and the necessity of atonement.

Everything changes when evil stands out against the background of the belief in human goodness: then it becomes a failure, a heresy. Now we are accountable for every infraction, every shortcoming, we are guilty of destroying the human race's good opinion of itself. And whereas some people will seek to do away with evil as a whole, like revolutionaries, or in part, like reformers, the suspicion arises that this project may be illusory and that misfortune will always shadow human experience. Even before the French Revolution married virtue with the scaffold and gave the lie to the dream of an ideal society, the whole eighteenth century had experienced the difficulty of achieving felicity. People thought they were beginning a countdown, doing away with iniquity, and then fell back into the same old ruts. *Decidedly, the old world did not want to die.* Even freed of its prejudices and ignorance, the human mind still registered a cleavage between values and facts.

Now, deprived of its religious alibis, suffering no longer means anything, it encumbers us like a terrible load of ugliness that we do not know what to do with. It is no longer explained but simply noted. It has become the enemy to be killed because it defies all our pretensions to establish a rational order on Earth. It used to generate redemption; now it is supposed to generate reparations. But by a strange paradox whose consequences we will discuss later, the more we try to eradicate suffering, the more it proliferates and multiplies. Then everything that resists the clear power of the understanding, the satisfaction of the senses, and the propagation of progress is called "suffering": the proclaimed society of happiness gradually becomes a society haunted by distress, pursued by the fear of death, illness, or aging. Masked by a smile, it detects everywhere an unbearable odor of disaster.

Finally, pleasure has no sooner been freed from its moralizing straitjacket than it encounters another major obstacle: boredom. To enjoy ourselves in complete serenity, it is not enough to do away with taboos and fears. Happiness corresponds to an economy, to calculations, to weighings; it needs varieties as much as contrasts. Satisfaction is as fatal to it as impediments. Here again Voltaire, both a pioneer and a critic, seems to have said everything there is to say. Man, he writes in *Candide*, is torn "between the turmoil of anxiety and the lethargy of boredom." And Julie, the heroine of Rousseau's epistolary novel *The New Héloïse*, goes even further: "All I see around me are reasons to be happy and I am not happy . . . I am too happy and I am bored" (part 6, letter 8). Scandalous remarks that put official euphoria in question without, however, rejecting it: happiness is delicate, not because it succumbs under the burden of prohibitions, but because it exhausts itself as soon as it is given free rein. And from the eighteenth century on, felicity and vacuity go hand in hand (an association already noted in antiquity).

In short, happiness has no sooner been baptized than it collides with two obstacles: it is diluted in ordinary life, and it encounters obstinate pain everywhere. In some respects, the Enlightenment assigned itself an immoderate goal: proving itself worthy of Christianity at its best. Stealing religions' prerogatives in order to outdo them: that was and is modernity's goal. And the great ideologies of the nineteenth and twentieth centuries (Marxism, socialism, fascism, liberalism) were perhaps no more than earthly substitutes for the great religions, intended to retain a minimum meaning for human suffering, without which suffering would become literally unbearable. Thus modernity remains haunted by the very thing that it claims to have transcended. What was supposed to have been left behind returns to obsess later generations in the form of remorse or nostalgia. That is why, as Chesterton brilliantly put it, the contemporary world is "full of old Christian virtues gone mad." Happiness is one of those virtues. At least the eighteenth century was the century not of arrogant well-being but of fragile well-being, of a perpetual hypersensitivity that is troubled not to discover in reality what it had hoped to find there. The twentieth century ceased to be as prudent.

CHAPTER 3

The Disciplines of Beatitude

Here, we are happy.

— Slogan in Castro's Cuba

The Dalai Lama is happy and breathes happiness.

—HIS HOLINESS THE DALAI LAMA and
   HOWARD CUTLER, *The Art of Happiness*

[The old man said,] "When I get up in the
morning, . . . I have two choices—either to be
happy or to be unhappy, and what do you think I
do? I just choose to be happy." . . . Lincoln . . . said
that people were just about as happy as they made
their minds up to be. Just choose happiness. . . . Say
to yourself, "Things are going nicely. Life is good.
I choose happiness," and you can be quite certain
of having your choice.

—NORMAN VINCENT PEALE,
   The Power of Positive Thinking

In 1929 Freud declared in his *Civilization and Its Discontents*
that happiness was impossible: it is the constantly growing part of his desires that the individual has to give up
in order to live in society, all cultures being based on the

renunciation of instincts. Noting that unhappiness threatens us from all sides, in our body, in nature, in our relations with others, Freud draws the following conclusion: "the intention that man should be 'happy' is not included in the plan of 'Creation.' What we call happiness in the strictest sense of the word comes from the (preferably sudden) satisfaction of needs which have been dammed up to a high degree, and it is from its nature only possible as an episodic phenomenon."[1]

Chimerical for the father of psychoanalysis, hardly fifty years later felicity has become virtually obligatory. In the meantime a dual revolution has taken place. Capitalism has ceased to be a system of production based on saving and labor and become a system of consumption that assumes expenditure and waste. A new strategy, which includes pleasure instead of excluding it, does away with the antagonism between the economic machine and our drives and makes the latter the engine of development. But above all, the Western individual has extricated himself from the straitjacket of the collectivity, from the first, authoritarian phase of democracies, and acquired full autonomy. Now that he is free, he no longer has a choice: since the obstacles on the road to Eden have vanished, he is "condemned" to be happy; or, to put it another way, he has only himself to blame if he isn't.

In the twentieth century the idea of happiness developed in two different directions. Whereas in democratic countries it manifested itself in a frenetic quest for pleasure

[1] Sigmund Freud, *Civilization and Its Discontents*, trans. J. Strachey (New York: Norton, 1962), p. 23.

(hardly fifteen years separate the liberation of Auschwitz from the emergence of consumerism in Europe and America), in the communist world it lapsed into the system of imposed happiness for everyone. How many mass graves have been dug in the name of the achieving the good, of making men better in spite of themselves? Put in the service of a political vision, happiness was a terrible tool for murder. To realize the radiant cities of tomorrow, no sacrifice, no extermination of human vermin seemed too great. The promised idyll turned into a horror.

We will not deal with that totalitarian deviation, the coercion of the kind Orwell described, or the emotional force-feeding Huxley imagined (even though many traits of our societies make us think of *1984* or *Brave New World*). Instead, we will examine another mechanism peculiar to the era of individualism that pertains to self-construction as an infinite task. It is as if order, having ceased to speak the language of law and effort, had decided to pamper us, help us; as if a kind of angel accompanied each of us and whispered in our ears: "Above all, don't forget to be happy." The counter-Utopias rebelled against a world that was too perfectly regulated, like a clock; now we carry the clock inside ourselves.

Voluntary Enchantments

By what perverse mechanism has a dearly won right become a law, and yesterday's prohibition become today's norm? Our whole religion of felicity is driven by the idea of mastery: we are supposed to be the masters of our destiny and all our delights, capable of constructing them and summoning them whenever we want. Happiness has been entered alongside technology and science in the list of Promethean exploits: we should produce it in the two-fold sense of the term, create it and display it. During the twentieth century this was asserted by a whole intellectual group that repeated in countless ways the same credo: happiness is a matter of will. In France the best example is the philosopher Alain, who, in his *Propos* written between 1911 and 1925 (which immediately became an uncontested best seller), identifies joy with physical exercise and melancholy with moodiness. Against jeremiads and moroseness, we have to "swear to be happy" and teach this art to children. People who choose to be cheerful and never complain should be rewarded.

Whatever the situation—stomachache, rainy day, empty purse—"it is a duty to others to be happy."[2] In Alain, this willed happiness pertains chiefly to the art of manners and politeness: it "is polite to be cheerful" (Marie Curie), to refrain from displaying one's misfortunes and to act as if everything is fine so as to maintain a pleasant sociability.

[2] Alain, *Propos sur le bonheur*. The expression "the duty to be happy" (*devoir de bonheur*) comes from Malebranche, who identifies it with spiritual improvement and makes the rehabilitation of self-esteem one of the instruments of salvation. It is used by Kant as a hypothetical imperative that prepares the reign of the moral law: "To secure one's own happiness is a duty, at least indirectly, for discontent with one's condition, under a pressure of many anxieties and amidst unsatisfied wants, could easily become a great temptation to transgression of duty" (*Fundamental Principles of the Metaphysics of Morals*, trans. T. K. Abbott). Finally, it is advocated by the utilitarians, who emphasize everyone's obligation to maximize one's potential in the name of pleasure.

That is why this civility of the agreeable is better suited to formulation as a maxim than as a system.

In his *Les Nourritures terrestres* (1897), André Gide presents a veritable manifesto of the joys of the flesh and the senses and advocates an ethic of fervor that privileges desire over satiety, thirst over its quenching, availability over possession. But in *Les Nouvelles Nourritures* (1935), this militant sensualist defends what was to become the credo of our age: the age of happiness as a right, the motto for a generation "that rises toward life fully armed with joy." "A sum of happiness is due each creature depending on how much his heart and his senses can take. If any part of it is refused me, I have been robbed."

Finally came the explosion of May 1968 and its proclamation that all desires were liberated. A year earlier, the movement had been anticipated by the situationist Raoul Vaneigem's book *Traité de savoir-vivre à l'usage des jeunes générations*,[3] in which he managed both to announce and to sum up the spirit of that period. Bubbling with fury and enthusiasm, Vaneigem blasts the condition in which humanity is vegetating because of a moribund and mercantile bourgeoisie. In opposition to this servitude, he advocates a free federation of subjectivities, which alone will allow "the intoxication of possibilities, the dizziness of all pleasures made accessible to all." We are indebted to Vaneigem not only for a call to engage in crime and a bloodbath to liquidate exploiters and the "organizers of boredom," but also for some of the finest slogans of May

---

[3] Paris: Gallimard, 1967.

1968: "We want nothing to do with a world in which a guarantee that you won't starve to death is exchanged for the certainty that you'll die of boredom," or again, this pathetic cry: "We were born never to grow old, never to die." It is an understatement to say that here Vaneigem, claiming to be the heir of Sade, Fourier, Rimbaud, and the surrealists, expresses a voluntarist view of existence: according to him, intensity is gained through a ruthless struggle between the spirit of submission and the forces of freedom. No half-measures: a dual battle against the slave within and the many masters who want to enslave us. Either life as a whole or absolute defeat: "Woe to him who abandons along the way his violence and radical demands. . . . in every renunciation, reaction prepares nothing less than our total death."

Those involved in May 1968 and Vaneigem himself vehemently rejected the word "happiness," which smelled of petit bourgeois silliness, the boring idylls of consumerism, and the psychology of mere opinion. Like the beatniks and hippies before them, they were protesting against a certain conformist joyfulness in the 1950s, incarnated by the American dream—a united family gathered around its car and its house in the suburbs, the combination of marriage and the refrigerator ecstatically celebrated by advertising. In 1945 Henry Miller, in a work of rare violence against America, had called this "the air-conditioned nightmare."[4] But with one of those winks of the eye that are customary in history, this revolt conducted in the name of desire

[4] Henry Miller, *The Air-conditioned Nightmare* (New York: New Directions, 1945).

coagulated in a new dogma of happiness: the insurrection was less against happiness itself than against an excessively restrictive definition of its attributes. Thus its content was renewed without killing it, and, as often happens, the main adversaries of the system turned out to be its best allies.

But the 1960s also reactivated an illusion that derived directly from the Enlightenment: that virtue and pleasure, morality and instinct, could be combined to lead humans effortlessly toward duty.[5] Happiness and the law are compatible, thinks the rationalistic optimism of the eighteenth century. Anyone who desires cannot be guilty, the 1960s and 1970s claimed; sin proceeds only from prohibitions. That was the illusion of a time that considered all inclinations equally respectable and believed in their harmonious convergence. No one suspected then that such a glorification of sovereign caprice and innocent desire, which alone decide what is good and what is evil, could justify the worst violence—something that Sade, who was more lucid than our modern libertines, clearly understood. We must also mention here the sublime and grotesque hope (propagated under one name or another by Groddeck, Reich, and Marcuse) that pleasure and orgasm are still the best ways not only to subvert society but to defy death and old age, which, Vaneigem maintained, proceed in no way from nature but rather from a "gigantic social bewitchment."

What began with Alain and grew steadily toward its culmination at the end of the twentieth century was the

---

[5] On the way in which natural law came to be conflated with the moral imperative, see Mauzi, *L'Idée de bonheur*, p. 145.

idea that we are moving from happiness as a right to happiness as an imperative. We are the heirs of these conceptions, even if we have not adopted any of them literally,
because they have crystallized in a common mentality
that imbues all of us today. Not only have pleasure, health,
and salvation become synonymous because the body is
now a horizon that cannot be transcended, but above all
the body has become suspect if it is not radiant. That is
a transgression of the taboo that commands everyone to
desire maximal self-fulfillment.

It will be objected that the twentieth century produced
other, darker conceptions of life: existentialism and the
philosophies of anguish, not to mention literature, which
kept a tragic vision alive. But these doctrines were all more
or less doctrines of liberation, of the solitary individual
giving himself his own law, without gods. The end of the
twentieth century, following a trend already observed in
the nineteenth, put freedom in the service of happiness,
not the other way around, and saw in happiness the apo-
gee of every emancipatory trajectory. Benjamin Constant
noticed this and defined Moderns' freedom as "security in
private pleasures" and a fierce concern with individual independence. The ideal of happiness was long opposed to
the bourgeois norm of success; now this same happiness
has become one of the ingredients of success. In the 1950s
Albert Camus could still defend the frantic taste for pleasure and nuptials with the world against the Stalinist vulgate
and French official prudery. Twenty years later this same
taste had become an advertising slogan. Now I have the

fearsome privilege of owing happiness as much to myself as to others. This right, of which I am myself the principal guarantee, credits me with a power over myself that thrills me but can also weigh on me like a burden: if enchantment depends on my choice alone, then I alone am guilty for my defeats. Does this mean that to feel good, all I have to do is will it, decree it, or program it in my own way?

Irrefutable Joys

Why did the critique of consumer society lead so quickly to the triumph of consumerism in the 1960s? Because the slogans shouted in those days—"We want everything right now," "Death to boredom," "Live constantly and enjoy without inhibitions"—applied less to the domain of love and life than to that of merchandise. People thought they were subverting the established order, but in fact they were, with the best of intentions, favoring the propagation of universal commercialism. It is in the domain of hunger and thirst that everything must be immediately available, whereas the heart and desire have their own rhythms, their intermittencies. The intention was to produce freedom, but the result was advertising: what was liberated was less our libido than our appetite for unlimited shopping, our ability to lay our hands on all goods without restriction. A fine image of the revolutionary as a regular prospector for capital—which is what the workers' movement, Marxism, and the radical Left finally turned out to be, capable of detecting a flaw in the system and allowing the latter to reform itself at less expense. A little like the hippies who discovered the favorite tourist sites in Asia,

Africa, and the Pacific thirty years before everyone else did, even though they were motivated by the desire to get away and find solitude.

Criticizing consumption is absurd, the luxury of spoiled children. There is this much to be said for consumption: it offers a simple, inexhaustible, accessible ideal for everyone, provided that one is solvent. All it requires is to want something and pay for it. We are stuffed, saturated like spoon-fed babies. Whatever one thinks of consumption, we enjoy it a great deal since, as in the case of fashion, we adopt passionately what is offered us as if we had chosen it ourselves. Since Charles Fourier we know that a pleasure cannot be refuted by anathemas; it has to be absorbed and supplanted by a greater pleasure. Does consumerism revolt you the way the sheep milling about in supermarkets and department stores revolt you? Then invent other joys, create new temptations! But for God's sake stop whining!

A Charitable Coercion

The liberation of mores was a strange venture, and even if we know this by heart, we never get tired of repeating it, and savoring its bitter reversal. For centuries the body was repressed, crushed in the name of religion or conventions, to the point that in the West it became the symbol of subversion. Now that it has been set free, something strange is happening: instead of enjoying pleasures in all innocence, we have relocated the prohibition within enjoyment itself. Pleasure, having become anxious about itself, has set up its own tribunal and condemns itself, no longer in the name of God or modesty, but because it is insufficient: it is never strong enough, never enough in compliance. Formerly irreconcilable enemies, morality and happiness have fused; today, it is being unhappy that is immoral; the superego has moved into the citadel of felicity and governs it with an iron hand. The end of culpability comes at the price of endless torment. Pleasure is no longer a promise but a problem. The idea of full satisfaction has replaced that of constraint, and it has in turn become a requirement that full satisfaction be achieved.[6] Each of us is responsible for being in good shape, in a good mood, and no longer has to renounce anything; instead, we have to adapt to a process of improvement that rejects any resistance to change. Order has ceased to condemn us or deprive us; now it shows us, with maternal solicitude, how to fulfill ourselves.

It would be a mistake to take this generosity for a liberation. Instead, it is a kind of charitable coercion that produces the malaise from which it later tries to free people. The statistics it publishes and the models it displays create a new race of offenders who are no longer sybarites or libertines but rather morose kill-joys, depressives. Happiness is no longer a stroke of good luck, a moment of splendor wrung from the monotony of the everyday, it is our condition, our destiny. When the desirable becomes

---

[6] According to a logic already discussed in Pascal Bruckner and Alain Finkielkraut, *Le Nouveau désordre amoureux* (Paris: Seuil, 1977), and further elaborated by others, notably Jean-Claude Guillebaud in *La Tyrannie du plaisir* (Paris: Seuil, 1998), who inquires into the role of prohibition in a modern society.

possible, it is immediately integrated into the category of the necessary. What used to be edenic is now ordinary. Social status is no longer determined solely by wealth or power, but also by appearance: it is not enough to be rich, you also have to look good, and this produces a new kind of discrimination and invidious comparison that is no less severe. There is a whole *ethic of seeming to feel good about oneself* that governs us and is supported by the smiling intoxication of advertising and merchandise.

Become your own best friend, acquire self-esteem, think positively, dare to live in harmony, etc.—the multitude of books on the subject suggests that it isn't so easy. Happiness not only constitutes, along with the market in spirituality, the biggest industry of the age; it is also and very precisely the new moral order, and that is why depression is spreading and every rebellion against this slimy hedonism constantly elicits unhappiness and distress. We are guilty of not being content, a problem for which we have to answer to everyone else and before our inner jurisdiction as well. Thus these fabulous polls worthy of the former Soviet bloc countries, in which 90 percent of the people questioned by a magazine say they are happy! No one would dare confess that he is sometimes unhappy for fear of diminishing his social standing.[7] The doctrine of pleasure strangely contradicts itself when it becomes militant and takes over prohibitions' power to exert pressure, merely reversing the direction. We are supposed to transform the uncertain expectation of delight into a

[7] Poll in the *Figaro-Magazine*, November 10, 1998.

summons addressed to ourselves, convert the difficulty of being into a permanent sweetness. Instead of admitting that happiness is an art of the indirect that is achieved or not through secondary goals, it is presented as if it were an immediately accessible objective, and recipes are provided. Whatever the method chosen, psychic, somatic, chemical, spiritual, or computer-based (there are people who see in the Internet something more than a splendid tool; they see it as the new Holy Grail, the realization of worldwide democracy[8]), the presupposition is everywhere the same: contentment is within your reach, all you have to do is undergo a "positive conditioning," an "ethical discipline" that will lead you to it.[9] This amounts to an astonishing inversion of the will, which seeks to establish its protectorate over psychic states and feelings that are traditionally outside its jurisdiction. It wears itself out trying to change what does not depend on it (at the risk of not dealing with what can be changed). Not satisfied with having entered into the general program of the welfare state and consumerism, happiness has also become a system in which everyone intimidates everyone else and of which we are both victims and accomplices. A terrorism consubstantial with those who are subject to it, since they have only one way of warding off attacks: making other people ashamed of their lacks and fragility as well.

[8] See Bertrand Leclair, *L'Industrie de la consolation* (Paris: Verticale, 1998).

[9] Dalai Lama, *The Art of Happiness*, p. 46. Moreover, in his conversations with Fabien Ouaki he says, "We have to construct a world in which children will be constantly immersed in a positive atmosphere." Fabien Ouaki, *La Vie est à nous* (Paris: Presses-Pocket, 1998), p. 145.

Health, Sexuality, Anxiety

Eros has the peculiarity of making love calculable and subjecting it to the power of mathematics; in the seclusion of the bedroom, lovers take the exam of happiness and ask themselves: are we up to snuff? It is from their sexuality, that new oracle, that they are asking tangible proofs of their passion. Combinations of the academic and gastronomic models: following a good recipe leads to getting a good grade. From caresses to positions, from perversions to thrills, they test their marriage or their relationship, draw up balance sheets of orgasm, compete with other couples in noisy demonstrations, exhibitionist confessions, give themselves prizes or honorable mentions, and try in this way to reassure themselves as to the state of their feelings. Erotic pleasure is not only an old audacity that the liberalization of mores has transformed into a commonplace: within the erosion and intermittencies of the heart it is the only thing on which people can count and that allows them to convert into memorable quantities the fleeting emotions passing through them. Thus they use the magic of numbers to evaluate the harmony of their relationships and check to be sure that the yield in pleasure is adequate.

In the same way, the obsession with health tends to medicalize every moment in life instead of allowing us to live in easy insouciance. This is manifested in the annexation to the therapeutic domain of everything that previously belonged to the order of savoir-vivre: collective rituals and pleasures are converted into anxieties, evaluated in terms of their utility or their harmfulness. Food, for example, is no longer divided into good and bad but into healthful and unhealthful. Food that meets certain standards is preferred to food that tastes good, regularly shaped fruit to irregularly shaped. The dining table is no longer the altar of succulent delights, a place for sharing a meal and conversation, but a pharmacy counter where we keep an eye on our fats and calories and conscientiously eat food reduced to a form of medication. We have to drink wine, not because we like it but to keep our arteries flexible, eat whole-grain bread to stay regular, and so on. The paradox is that the country where this hygienic obsession is most widespread, the United States, is also the country of fast food and epidemic obesity. What matters most is no longer living to the full the time that is granted us but extending it as much as possible: the notion of the stages of life has been replaced by that of longevity.

Duration becomes a canonical value even if it has to be won at the price of terrible restrictions. For example, an emaciated American student who eats only one meal a day in order to reach the canonical age of 140 and admits that he is terribly depressed. Or the fanatics of life prolongation who take as many as eighty pills a day in order to make it past the fateful barrier of one hundred years. Making time, which used to mean reserving a few moments for one's own ends, is now associated with an unremitting productivism, a maniacal accumulation of additional years of life. There is no question that extraordinary advances in extending longevity have been achieved, though it is less life that is being prolonged than old age, which is drawn out indefinitely at the risk of swelling the population of older people to continental dimensions and giving the West a geriatric face (that is why the cult of youth is an ideology of aging nations). But our pitiful excursions toward the promised land of great health are comparable to the self-mortifications that used to be practiced by religious zealots. By trying to eliminate every anomaly, every weakness, we end up denying the principal virtue of health: a lack of concern about oneself or, as Leriche put it, the "silence of the organs" (even if the latter may be deceptive). The hair shirt is not worn to restrain the impulses of rebellious flesh, but rather to punish an imperfect body for not corresponding to the ideal model. This is the outcome of the old Christian prediction of immortality and the resurrection of "glorious bodies" that are incorruptible, will never rot or wither, and are found in science fiction. Our wild scientific fantasies come directly from religion, of which they claim to be the fulfillment.

Only a sick person can think that "health is happiness."[10] For someone who is not sick, health is just a fact and nothing more. To make health the equivalent of felicity is to imply that we are all moribund without knowing it, and that we need to be made aware of our condition. Now we always have to save ourselves from something—high blood pressure, imperfect digestion, a tendency to gain weight; we are never thin enough, muscular enough, tanned enough. The therapeutic ideal has become an obsession that accompanies us everywhere and that the media and

[10] Advertisement in the periodical *Santé Magazine*, January 2000.

those around us never let us forget. In the name of this norm, which is further aggravated by predictive medicine and genetic screening, we are all becoming potential invalids, fearfully examining our excess pounds, our cardiac rhythms, and the elasticity of our skins. A strange, obstinate self-examination and self-castigation that make the body the site of a latent menace, just as it used to be in Christianity (Baudrillard). But we are now threatened less by hellfire than by the softening and sagging of our physical appearance. And since being in good shape is a sign of election, just as wealth used to be for Calvinists the reward for those who worked hard, letting yourself go becomes, inversely, a synonym of decline, of being ready for the scrap heap. Whence the frequent comparison of our fitness clubs and their machines with medieval instruments of torture—except that in our case we are all voluntary victims. Bodybuilding illustrates the dream of re-creating one's own anatomy, with the astonishing paradox that an excess of muscles tends to make the body look as if it were skinned or turned inside out like a glove, as if to show, with all its visible veins and tendons, the outrage that has been done it.

Farewell to Insouciance

Thus health annexes all areas of life: in 1978 the World Health Organization defined it as "complete physical, mental, and social well-being." We are supposed to use every means we can to achieve it, including spiritual methods. Here we find a magic reconciliation of all values: it's good for you to be kind,[11] compassion boosts the level of immunoglobulin A, an antibody that helps combat respiratory infections, increases life expectancy, and attenuates depression;[12] peace of mind attracts friendship and money;[13] believing in God is good for your health and those who believe live longer—all this is scientifically proven![14] Whence the unlimited demand for

[11] "The compassion I show does me good in return. It is the best kind of protection, and I am the primary beneficiary. It provides inner peace, bodily health, and happy days, and a long life. Not to mention lives to come." Dalai Lama and Jean-Claude Carrière, *La Force du bouddhisme* (Paris: Presses-Pocket, 1998), p. 129. This is one of the rare books of interviews with 'His Holiness" in which the interviewer far surpasses the interviewee.

[12] Dalai Lama and Howard Cutler, *The Art of Happiness*, pp. 126–127, notes:

> David McClelland, a psychologist at Harvard, showed a group of students a film of Mother Teresa working among Calcutta's sick and poor. The students reported that the film stimulated feelings of compassion. Afterward, he analyzed the students' saliva and found an increase in immunoglobulin-A, an antibody that can help fight respiratory infections. In another study done by James House at the University of Michigan Research Center, investigators found that doing regular volunteer work, interacting with others in a warm and compassionate way, dramatically increased life expectancy, and probably overall vitality as well. . . . Studies have shown that reaching out to help others can induce a feeling of happiness, a calmer mind, and less depression.

[13] "Therefore I make peace of mind primary: if your mind is at peace, health will follow: peaceful people generally attract good companions and a happy disposition generally attracts money. In any case, someone whose mind is at peace will use money correctly." Ouaki, *La Vie est à nous*, p. 26. Ouaki is president of the Tati clothing store chain.

[14] According to the Dalai Lama and Howard Cutler, *The Art of Happiness*, p. 304:

> Extensive recent investigations seem to confirm that religious faith can substantially contribute to a happier life. Those conducted by independent researchers and polling organizations . . . have found that religious people report feeling happy and satisfied with life more often that nonreligious people. Studies have found that . . .

medical, pharmaceutical, aesthetic, and mystical benefits, the conversion of medication into a prosthesis intended to increase our satisfaction, slow the deterioration of our senses, and lessen anguish. These amount to perfectly licit drugs analogous to *soma* in Aldous Huxley's *Brave New World*; like Prozac and melatonin, they are supposed to regulate our moods, protect us from adversity, and keep us young until we die.[15] At the risk, characteristic of miracle remedies, of making discontent illegitimate and having problems a sign of infirmity (just as the use of Viagra when it is not medically required suggests that the body must be capable of peak sexual performance at all times). Here we are far from the classical wisdom that offered an abundance of advice for dealing with everyday problems: Alain still recommended ways of stopping a cough, curing hiccups, getting something out of your eye, and not being bored while traveling by train. Practical techniques

---

religious faith also appears to help individuals deal more effectively with issues such as aging or coping better with personal crises and traumatic events. In addition, statistics show that families of those with strong religious belief often have lower rates of delinquency, alcohol and drug abuse, and ruined marriages. There is even some evidence to suggest that faith may have benefits for people's physical health—even for those with serious illnesses. There have been . . . epidemiological studies establishing a link between strong religious faith, lower death rates, and improved health.

[15] William Regelson, a professor at Virginia Commonwealth University's medical school and a promoter of melatonin, imagines the following scenario of future happiness: "It's your birthday. You love your work but you've canceled your afternoon appointments to celebrate. You're going to play squash with a friend and then you'll join your wife at a jazz club. You've reserved the honeymoon suite, where there is a Jacuzzi. The next day you're going to go Rollerblading in the park with your great-grandchildren: this is no longer your grandchildren's futuristic scenario but your own life." Quoted by Sarah Daniel in *Le Nouvel observateur*, 1995.

in a circumscribed domain that did not pretend to embrace the totality of life. But chemistry, which is all the more seductive because its achievements are immense and incontestable, offers us "portable ecstasies" (Thomas de Quincey on opium), the sovereign good in the form of a little pill.

Health has its martyrs, pioneers, heroes, and saints, but in every case we pay a price for it both financially and psychologically in the form of all sorts of monitoring and surveillance. *It prevents us from ever forgetting ourselves,* since sickness and recovery are becoming less and less distinct, at the risk of creating a society of hypochondriacs and permanently "dysfunctional" persons. The only crime we can commit against it is not to think about it day and night. From childhood on, we are required to redeem our imperfection, to reshape ourselves from head to toe. This work done on ourselves, this incessant inspection, even if it has to do with matters as futile as tanning or losing weight in preparation for a vacation at the beach, is the equivalent of a moral redemption. Our professors of well-being, whether clerics, psychologists, philosophers, or physicians, are kind inquisitors who manage to dry up our main source of joy: detachment, insouciance, unawareness of little everyday problems. (This is what we call the state of grace: a moment of enchantment when we keep the howling pack of torments at a distance and when chance and good luck coalesce and shower their benefits on us.) Whereas during the Middle Ages death hovered over every living person and could strike at any time, today, thanks to science, everyone has the potential to be immortal; but how many sorrows and sacrifices have to be endured in order to gain a few years or to enter the "paradise" of those who live to be a hundred years old. Perhaps someday we will have to demand, against the new dogma of immortality, the right to die as our ancestors did, very simply.

The anguish resides in the fear of not being able to keep up, of lacking vim and vigor in this highly competitive world. We judge ourselves, punish ourselves like meticulous spiritual advisors. The majority conception of happiness has long since moved beyond the soppy, rose-colored realm of popular literature; it has become hard, demanding, and inflexible as well.[16] This is a mortification that comes to us in the guise of affability and indulgence and commands us never to be satisfied with our condition. The severe visage of the old preachers has been replaced by the omnipresent smile of the new ones. Therapy with a smile: that is the incontestable market advantage Buddhists have over Christians. That is why Buddhism is making inroads among the rich in temperate countries, whereas Protestants and Catholics are converting poor people in the tropics.

We may also wonder about the Dalai Lama's success in the Western media, which contrasts with his relative political failure. In choosing to popularize Buddhism in

---

[16] That is why the typical contemporary ailment is, as Jean Cazeneuve pointed out, a crisis of adjustment to prefabricated happiness; not spleen or melancholy, but ulcers and heart attacks. Cazeneuve, *Bonheur et civilisation* (Paris: Gallimard, 1962), p. 202. Similarly, Alain Ehrenberg has shown convincingly how depression, anxiety, and inhibition arise from the fatigue of being oneself. Ehrenberg, *Fatigue d'être soi* (Paris: Odile Jacob, 1998).

order to defend the Tibetan cause, he may have arrived at a contradiction: he has succeeded in making the former fashionable by adapting it and toning it down, but he has emptied the latter of meaning. Coming out of exile like an Asian Moses descending from his Himalayas to reveal the essential truths to us, the bearer of an extraordinary history and culture and a marvelous tradition, in the course of time he has transformed himself into a worldly guru (like Rajneesh and Maharishi Mahesh Yogi before him, and like Deepak Chopra today, who has become a mentor to Hollywood stars[17]), part marriage counselor, part dietician, and part spiritual advisor, tolerantly and good-naturedly offering abundant answers, for he has an answer to every question. It is as if he had become, probably without being aware of it, a pure product of marketing, a sort of peddler specializing in wisdom and serenity, and punctuating each of his remarks with his legendary laugh. As an official supplementary soul for a materialistic West (the heart being Abbé Pierre or the late Mother Teresa), he provides amiable twaddle precisely calibrated to the taste of European and American audiences. His peculiar talent is to have invented, like Paulo Coelho, a worldwide spiritual Esperanto that is accessible to everyone without barriers or constraints, a chameleon-like discourse that can be adapted to any audience whatever. This champion of the monastic ideal is the object of a cult that amounts almost

---

[17] Deepak Chopra has published, among other books, *Ageless Body, Timeless Mind* (New York: Harmony, 1999), in which he defends the notion that senility, infirmity, and death belong to the past, whereas a new reality centered on creativity, joy, achievement, and eternal vigor is now opening up.

to idolatry, especially among his Western disciples; confronted by him, these ardent scourgers of Judeo-Christian obscurantism lose all critical sense, all distance, prostrating themselves before him and going into unbridled ecstasies. What is surprising is not that the Dalai Lama seduces people—he has what it takes to do that, and the Tibetan saga is as fabulous as the Chinese occupation is abject— but that he has succumbed to this success with an almost childlike jubilation and can never get enough in the way of publicity, speaking engagements, and interviews. With this hammy prophet we are very far from the ethical and historical grace of a Mahatma Gandhi or a Martin Luther King Jr., those great apostles of nonviolence. The Dalai Lama came to introduce the Orient, and we have made him a performer in our own image. In the religious supermarket, he has hoisted himself to the top, dethroning the pope, pastors, rabbis, patriarchs, and imams, all of them much too rebarbative. Things may change, but I am not sure that Buddhism and the Tibetan people have gained much through this promotion.

People with Perpetual Bad Luck

Given a choice between two options, they always choose the worse and show an unheard-of talent for blundering into all kinds of hornets' nests. When they go on vacation, they are immediately robbed or catch the rarest virus in the region. Every time a holiday comes around, they are bitter and upset, as if they felt personally insulted by the collective joy. They somehow manage to fail at everything they try and "make their own unhappiness" (Paul Watzlawick) with a consistency and success rate that we can only admire. Their lives quickly come to resemble a rubble heap that confirms them in the conviction that they are predestined. There is a kind of black humor in the way they move automatically from one misfortune to another, as do sick people who collect the most atrocious pathologies to the point of constituting an anthology of morbidity all by themselves. Passionate creators of their own disasters, they set forth each detail with a refinement that amounts almost to art. Their deaths will be a ridiculous as their lives—atrocious, of course, but without grandeur.

Do they suffer from a failure neurosis? That is not clear. The chronically unfortunate person seeks, as we all do, to be recognized; and bad luck is the only signature he can put on the world. He has acquired through hard-fought struggle the right to bad-mouth life, and life pays him back in spades. This poor devil is comfortable only in catastrophes: good news would throw him into confusion. Unlike most of us, who have both good and bad moments, his constancy in misfortune fills him with a paradoxical pride, subtly designates him as one of the elect. He may have fallen, but in the depth of his wretchedness he is seated on a magnificent throne: the throne of the rejected.

The Via Dolorosa of Euphoria

The new, implacable happiness combines two kinds of intimidation: the discriminating power of a norm and the unforeseeable power of grace. It is a blessing all the more

insidious that it is never certain, and its provisional ben-
eficiaries—the beautiful, the happy, the fortunate—can
be dispossessed of it at any moment. The small number
of the elect is opposed to the great mass of the rejected,
heretics who are stigmatized as such. A command that is
all the fiercer because it is approximate and recedes as we
bow down before it. You have to suffer to display the car-
nivorous grin of the victors who had to fight to get where
they are and fear being dethroned in turn. Moreover, the
role of men's and women's periodicals is to issue regular
reminders of this precept. These periodicals, which are
simultaneously recreational, educational, and coercive—
or, to use their language, "amusing, practical, and fun"—
constantly hammer home two contradictory claims: that
beauty, a good figure, and pleasure are within your reach
if you are willing to pay the price. But if you are not, you
alone will be to blame when you get old and ugly and fail
to enjoy life. The democratic aspect: no one is any longer
doomed by his physical defects, nature is no longer destiny. The punitive aspect: never think you are done, you
can always do better; if you let up even a little, you will
plunge back into the hell of the soft, the out of shape, the
frigid.[18] Page after page, these periodicals—called "light"
even though they are terribly severe—whisper categorical
imperatives that are discreet but full of meaning: not content to provide us with models of men and women who are
constantly getting younger and more perfect, they suggest
a tacit contract: do as I tell you and you might come closer

[18] Thus the cover of the magazine *Biba* for July 1999: "Pleasure comes first!
Yes, yes, you can do better!"

to the sublime beings depicted in each issue. They play on very natural fears of getting old, ugly, fat and calm them only the better to arouse them.[19]

As long as it remained a "superb article of faith" (Cicero), happiness could fire our imagination, remain the vanishing point for a desire that remained alive and voracious. Now that it has become the only horizon of our democratic societies, being connected with work, will, and effort, it is necessarily a source of anguish. The fact that redemption is now to be had through the body and no longer solely through the soul changes nothing: we have to redeem ourselves for being what we are; no matter how old, the body is still a faulty mechanism in need of repair. In any case, our happiness worries us and poisons our lives with all sorts of demands that are impossible to meet. Like those high royal officials in Thailand who, as they lie on their deathbeds, are supposed to ask the king to give them permission to die and to provide flowers and incense, we leave it up to the peddlers of beatitude to tell us if we are following the right path. Our hedonism, far from being a pure Epicureanism or an orgiastic Dionysian revel, is full of disgrace and failure. No matter how closely

[19] One example among many: the magazine *Men's Health* (May–June 1999) included the following articles: five clever ways of slimming down; how to prolong the sex act for more than three minutes; how to keep your libido in good shape, how to survive a plane crash, a heart attack, or marital problems; how to diagnose the condition of your own prostate; how to make love every day right up to your dying day, etc. Beneath the humor of the titles, we can discern a little refrain that becomes nightmarish. We think we are reading a sexy magazine and we find a catalog of potential offenses that casts a shadow of doubt on all the instruments of pleasure. Here amusement is inseparable from reformation.

we adhere to the rules, our bodies continue to betray us, age puts its stamp on us, sickness strikes us at will, and pleasures come and go according to a rhythm unaffected by our vigilance or resolution. We neither control nor possess our happinesses, which never come on schedule and then pop up when we are not expecting them. And our determination to purge or disinfect every physical or mental fragility—sorrow, despondency, off days—encounters our limits and our inertia, which does not allow itself to be shaped like putty. In other words, it is in our power to avoid and to correct certain evils. But just as peace is not merely an absence of war but a positive state (Spinoza), happiness is not the absence of adversity. It is a different kind of emotional quality that depends neither on our goodwill nor on our subtlety. We can be unafflicted without necessarily being euphoric. Amid great havoc we can have moments of unprecedented ecstasy.

Happiness experienced as a malediction: that is the dark side of the American dream to which so many books testify. Working to re-create paradise on Earth, far from the world's disorders, and then finding that it, too, is impure and contaminated, that "the promised land is always already compromised" (Jankélévitch). But this dream burns out only the better to rise again from its ashes: in spite of themselves, those who attack it reactivate its promise. Our societies put into the category of the pathological what other cultures consider normal—the preponderance of pain—and put into the category of the normal and even the necessary what others see as exceptional—the feeling of happiness. The question is not whether we are more or less happy than our ancestors: our conception of happiness has changed, and to change utopias is to change constraints. But we are probably living in the world's first societies that make *people unhappy not to be happy*.

A good example of "the disconcerting ease with which the pursuit of an ideal can lead to its contrary" (Isaiah Berlin). Cursed by joy, the galley slaves of pleasure, we have succeeded in using the weapons of paradise to re-create little hells. By insisting that each of us must be delighted or be condemned to social death, we have transformed hedonism into punishment and blackmail and subjected ourselves to the yoke of a despotic felicity. In this configuration, unhappiness takes on the fantastic dimension of what is denied and nonetheless subsists: it becomes a ghost, a specter that terrorizes us all the more because we are unable to give it a name. Let us leave those intoxicated by Eden to their dogmas and diktats. Here the point is only to exonerate, to lighten the burden: let everyone be left free not to be happy without feeling ashamed, or to be happy episodically as one sees fit. Issue no decisions, make no laws, impose nothing. If we do not want a legitimate aspiration to degenerate into a collective punishment, we must treat the pitiless idol of happiness with the most extreme disrespect.

PART II

The Kingdom of the Lukewarm, or The Invention of Banality

CHAPTER FOUR

The Bittersweet Saga of Dullness

The litter where the happy human cattle lie.

—MALLARMÉ

It is said that in London there is a very exclusive club that requires its members, on pain of being ejected, to utter only clichés. Anyone who tries to raise the level of conversation or expresses an idea of even the slightest interest is immediately expelled. A perilous exercise that requires no less agility of mind than does a legal plea or an oratorical contest.

Here, we are not concerned with this obligation to stick to platitudes, this descent of people, things, and discourses into a common world that makes them all equivalent.[1] Instead, we are concerned with another kind of banality that precedes any distinction between the banal and the original and arises from the turning point in the medieval world: a new system of time characterized by the prosification of the world, by the victory of the profane over the sacred. Religion, as it was practiced until the French Revolution, fulfilled a dual function: it gave direction to

[1] The expression that forms the title for part 2 is borrowed from Victor Segalen.

earthly existence and magnified its least brilliant aspects. Human time led us toward eternity through a series of tests like those encountered by John Bunyan's Pilgrim, who travels from the City of Destruction to the Celestial City, evading pitfalls like Vanity Fair and the Slough of Despond (*Pilgrim's Progress*, 1678). The perspective of the beyond made it possible to redeem the humblest, most miserable aspects of the human condition. The slightest pettiness was saved; the whole universe, in its ugliness and emptiness, was destined for deliverance.

Deliverance and Burden

When man substitutes himself for God as the foundation of law, and religion withdraws from the public sphere to become a private matter, time gains a certain autonomy. It is no longer solely a path toward the eternal, and whether it goes somewhere depends on us alone. It becomes an environment in which the individual can blossom and construct himself, but it also becomes a mire in which he can get bogged down; he is both a creator and a driveler. That is the modern discovery: life is not as repetitive as people say it is; new things can be invented, but life also repeats itself dreadfully. The "violent pathos of medieval life" (Huizinga) gives way to the indetermination of a temporal duration that is both fertile and tedious.

The withdrawal of the divine has a good side and a bad side: it provides human independence with a chance to develop itself freely, but the burden of everyday life has somehow to be borne alone. Only God, through continual creation, made it possible for things to persevere in their being and to avoid "lapsing back into their initial nothingness" (St. Augustine). Once God had withdrawn or been reduced to the role of the Great Clockmaker (and the proliferation of proofs of his existence up to the time of Kant shows just how problematic his existence had become), the universe no longer had any justification. Without their divine preserver, things reveal their arbitrariness, their tenuousness, the fact that "they are what they are" (Hegel). The medieval sublime yields to modern triviality, the great absolute to the merely relative. The terrible dizziness experienced by people whose chains have been struck off and who are less demystified than disoriented: they see that they are free, but they are pygmies. Emancipated from the feudal power that assigned them roles at birth and from the religious law that riveted them to the concern for salvation, they no longer know either predestination or destination.

But with this liberation is born banality, that is, humanity's total immanence in itself. The only possible way out is the future, and the sky hangs low and heavy over our heads. We find ourselves doomed to be only of this world; we are put under house arrest here below. Parodying Paul Morand, we might say: there is nothing but the Earth and its extended suburb, the cosmos. Ceasing to be enriched by the expectation of a better life, our planet shrivels up. With religion, the goal was to atone for one's sins and win salvation. Now the goal is to atone for the fact of existing at all. In the West, for more than a millennium the question was how to live in accord with God; we have gradually substituted another question that goes back to the concerns of the ancients: how to live, period.

The emotional confrontation with God, the biblical dramaturgy that resembles the lovers' duet, domestic disputes, and appearance before the divine tribunal—all that is over. Left alone with themselves, people have to relearn everything: the simple facts of being born, maturing, and growing old become problematic. There is no longer anything to save us from the prosaic element that used to constitute that modest part of existence that prayers, faith, and rituals could amend. If we have to free ourselves now, it is from this sticky dailiness; and we contrast less sin to grace than the ordinary to the exceptional. A new battle begins against time, the uncontested but elusive master, as if the human race had been liberated from the desire for eternity only to fall under the sway of profane time.

The emergence of the Enlightenment is inseparable, not from a dark side, as has been too often claimed, but from a gray area that the great ideologues will never be able to efface by means of their horizontal transcendence. Whence the two avenues that pleasure takes: either exhilaration, the boundless quest for intensity, or dullness, paradoxical delight in the insipid in its countless forms. That is why modernity and democracy are associated with the notions of mediocrity, stinginess, and triviality, those new divinities of the universal petit bourgeois. This is the adventure upon which the West has embarked: relegating religious belief to the depths of the heart, claiming the planet as the property of humanity alone, desacralizing it in order to exploit it rationally and scientifically. But in this gigantic construction project, in this extraordinary frenzy of invention and discovery, the grit of banality slips in everywhere, clogging the machinery and poisoning souls and destinies. A grotesque heteronomy is imposed, a heteronomy that is no longer that of God but of *dead scraps of time*, of erosion in the course of passing time. Banality is the destiny of humans without a destiny, an opportunity as well as a servitude that falls to each and every one of us. That is what has brought hell, paradise, and purgatory back to us, allowing us all to experience them successively or simultaneously in the course of our lives.

The Christian drama of salvation and perdition is the counterpart of the secular drama of success and failure. No one escapes it. Everything is determined during the brief span of a lifetime, without remission, without the consolation of a back-world that would provide relief for our present and past sufferings. A life, all the more poignant because there is only one and because in it the temporary takes on the character of the definitive. But who determines the criteria of failure or victory, who sets the official norms? What authority will separate the elect from the damned? As Dante said, "the straight way was lost." And who can assure us that a life that has failed, according to the rules currently in force, was not nonetheless a happy one? In the background here we can glimpse the malaise that was affected by the wealthy classes as early as the eighteenth century and that spread to the masses (that is perhaps the fate of democracy: to extend all the sufferings of the elites but without their privileges). As if restored to itself and to its powers, the whole of existence became a superhuman task. It is "very, very dangerous to live even one day" (Virginia Woolf, *Mrs. Dalloway*).

The Transfiguration of Routines

What is a habit? An energy-saving technique. It arises from the principle of conservation: not having to redo everything every morning, creating reflexes to absorb the incidental, the particular. A life without habits would be a nightmare because habit has become a second nature that spares us repeated effort. It is habit that allows us to master an art or craft that at first repelled us. We cling to our habits because they impress their rhythm on our lives and constitute their backbone. They are not simply routines; they also attest to our fidelity to ourselves. To renounce them would be to renounce ourselves. The great art consists not in breaking routines but in juggling several so as not to be dependent on any one of them. And it takes all our old habits to invent a new one. That is what we call a renaissance.

There is even a certain pleasure in repetition, whose ultimate trick consists in effacing itself, remaining unperceived at the very moment when it alone reigns. In repetition, time disappears by coming constantly back to the same. Obsessed with originality, the West cultivates an excessively negative view of the repetitive. There are cultures in which the return of the same theme, as in Arab and Indian music, or the immobility of a note held indefinitely, ends up creating imperceptible differences. Apparently monotone melodies are fraught with tiny variations. They compete with silence and hypnotize us by this strange way of moving forward and remaining stationary.

In the end, it is not regularity that kills life but our incapacity to magnify it into an art of living that spiritualizes what is basically biological and raises the smallest moment to the level of a ceremony. That is perhaps what distinguishes the two parts of the Western world, even if they are tending to merge. Americans, as worthy utilitarians, believe in happiness; they inscribed it in their Declaration of Independence and are prepared to teach it, prescribe it, to everyone. Whereas Europeans are more skeptical and prefer pleasures and especially *savoir-vivre*, which, shaped by a long tradition, forms a kind of collective civility including both joys and sorrows.

Consider the contrast between fast food—quick, solitary, and cheap—and gastronomy—convivial and time consuming. These are two ways of approaching time: either kill it, doing away with anything repetitive, or make it an ally by raising it to the level of a liturgy. One way depends on a service society organized around convenience and immediacy, the other on a customary society that sees its heritage and its customs as treasures of intelligence and finesse that it would be criminal to forget. The Old World's charm consists in the diversity of its cultures, which resist global leveling. The New World's magnetism consists in its reflex of systematic innovation. In one case, to be born is to be preceded, to be the heir to long-term knowledge; in the other, it is to cancel one's predecessors and leap forward toward the promised land of the future.

The truth is that both solutions tempt us, and we would like to benefit from the pleasures of the past without its constraints, and of the advantages of the present without its impoverishment. Children of a mixed heritage, we oscillate between nostalgia for ritual and fantasies of great simplification.

Frenetic Inertia

In 1998 a young woman in Washington, D.C., Jennifer Ringley, created a website that made it possible to observe her going about her ordinary tasks in her home, twenty-four hours a day. Setting aside the exhibitionism involved in such a project, which has since been repeated by many others, we can note that only a contemporary could imagine filming herself day after day, especially when there is nothing unusual about her life. There is a certain austerity, a commitment in this exercise in mechanical restitution. Here, the video assumes the role previously played by the diary; but whereas writing is necessarily selective, the camera registers everything: a garbage pail filling up, a bathtub emptying out, lettuce growing, a pair of slippers, not to mention the exciting episodes of going to bed, getting up, sleeping. What is astonishing is the importance accorded to this dreadful routine, the fascination with inanity. Maybe we should see in this a desire to redeem the tedium of the day-to-day, week-to-week, by putting it before the collective eye of thousands of Internet users, and also to reassure ourselves by seeing that we are all in the same boat: the boat of everyday life. As if we constituted the virtual community of people to whom nothing ever happens, the digital tribe of those deprived of events.

One can say two contradictory things about the everyday: it repeats itself and it exhausts us. It submerges us in the return of the same, makes tomorrow a copy of today, which itself reproduces yesterday with the persistence of a scratched phonograph record. Its laws are as rigorous as those of the cosmos. Conformity, normality, uniformity: the predominance of the *déjà vu*, the already lived, the triumph of the colorless and odorless, the endless cycle of the identical. It restores an eternal present with neither future nor past, as if all days had fused into one. The paradox is that it abolishes time by means of time itself, by being a grotesque of eternity, as a watch makes eternity by means of perpetual movement.[2] It has a power of erosion that takes the edge off the most terrible events; everything is swallowed up in it. That is why most of the metaphors of boredom are metaphors of bogging down, of seizing up, or coagulating: in Baudelaire and Poe, an icebound ship immobilized forever; in Flaubert, a dormant marsh; in Mallarmé, a sterile, frozen lake that paralyzes the swan; in Verlaine, a dreary plain covered with snow in winter; in Moravia, a calcium deposit that ends up obstructing the pipes; in Sartre, a viscosity as sticky as glue. For a long time the provinces, as a metaphysical as well as a geographical category (especially in very centralized countries like Russia and France), represented this low-flying life, this endless hibernation whose emptiness literature has been trying to describe for the past two centuries. A stunted, gray life, forever out of the loop, in which whole generations wall themselves up as if in a mausoleum. A vegetative state, an anticipatory mourning in which people renounce everything on Earth that is sweet, pleasant, moving, even before they have experienced anything, loved anything. In France the expression *la province* itself

---

[2] Gilles Lapouge, *Utopies et civilisations* (Paris: Albin Michel, 1973), pp. 110, 111.

fell into disuse with the end of the Jacobin model and the emergence of "regions."

The everyday, a realm of sempiternal repetition, makes everything neutral, does away with contrasts, flattens, and constitutes a power of indetermination that drowns loves, feelings, angers, and hopes in a gelatinous indifferentiation. That is why it contradicts any hope of ordering up happiness the way one might order up a meal: the everyday dissolves happiness, digests it, and deprives it of savor as soon as it appears. It is a machine that maintains itself and functions without any external fuel. Rising, getting dressed, feeding oneself, going to work—these simple acts require superhuman courage. "I know an Englishman," Goethe said, "who hanged himself so he wouldn't have to knot his tie every morning." A work, a project, has to be ripped out of the lifelessness of the passing days, out of their compact mass, and a true love is one that takes the risk of the everyday, dares to challenge it and does not retreat too soon, damaged or defeated. The everyday lacks the emotional attraction par excellence: suspense. In the everyday, nothing is expected, nothing thrills, because everything is repeated ad infinitum. The terrible repetition of the question "What's new?" and the answer "Nothing." Whereas for Baudelaire remorse is the inability to undo something, banality is, conversely, the inability to do anything, to inaugurate something new, to open a breach in the monotone mass of identical moments. Moreover, this stay-at-home world does not lack attractions for someone who wants to let himself float through life like a boat on a river, letting the dates on the calendar and the passage of the seasons direct him. There is a sedative pleasure to this routine: everything goes without saying; it clothes in the garb of necessity what was initially gratuitous. We are in a virtually automatic system. The fear that Sundays and vacations arouse in some people—the fear of a great void that has to be filled—arises from this momentary suspension of a regularity that may be exhausting but is also reassuring. However, for most people the curse of everyday life is that it is with us twenty-four hours a day, whereas we would like to cut into it at will, eat a few slices, and skip the rest. "O life, I love you, but not every day" (Cerroli), an admirable phrase that says it all.

The everyday also includes an agitated emptiness: its turmoil tires us, its monotony disgusts us. Nothing is happening to me, but this nothing is still too much: I am scattered among countless useless tasks, sterile formalities, and meaningless chatter that do not compose a life but suffice to exhaust me. That is what we call stress, the continuous corrosion within the lethargy that eats away at us day after day. As if meaninglessness itself demanded its tribute. Beneath the deceptive calm of our faded lives, an insidious war is being waged, in which anxiety and care throw us into a state of *tension without intention*. A laughable suffering that gnaws at each of us but does not constitute a tragedy. "Life leaks away through the brain and the nerves. . . . Modern nervousness is a cry of distress on the part of an organism battling with its environment" (Rosolino Coella). The countless discomforts endured do not even form an event, but they suffice to plunge us into a state that is typically modern: fatigue. *An abstract fatigue* that does not result from particular efforts because it arises from the simple fact of living, a fatigue that we would be wrong to try to drive away by resting because it is itself produced by routine. The everyday or permanent requisition: a command always to answer "present," at the office, in the car, in the family, and even in our dreams. What better example of this urgent demand than the cell phone: as soon as it rings we feel compelled to dig through our pockets or purses to catch the noisy, vibrating brute. Moreover, the whole development of technology leads to the social exclusion of those who do not keep up with it. You have to subscribe or perish, especially if you are a teenager.

These are just so many calls to arms and recruitments that take us away from ourselves, keep us constantly mobilized. Armed with his cell phone, his iPod, his headphone, and, no doubt soon, microchips in his brain and screens in his eyes, the new prosthetic human being, always ready for battle, connected to the whole world, is like a soldier waging an endless war. Exhaustion and overwork, our modern vices, Nietzsche called them. Forever fighting phantoms, we are the victims of incalculable damage, the seriously injured veterans of dullness. And there is a striking contrast between the thrilling changes and rapid development in the world as pictured in the media and the humdrum sameness of our individual existences. Everything is humming with exploits and drama, and my life is so flat. By a strange paradox, banality appears to us in the guise of disorder, and neurasthenia sets in masked by speed and agitation.

Stress is the opposite of adventure; it is the concentration necessary to maintain the everyday at its low level. Now we are struggling in a "frenetic inertia" (George Steiner), in a busyness that does not produce the unpredictable. We have all the disadvantages of dispersion and none of the advantages of the aleatory, none of the benefits of a genuine surprise. We stagnate in a median condition that is neither joy nor suffering: instead of feeling time shape us, we watch the days flow away "like blood from a wound" (Louis Guilloux). And we sometimes wish for a good disaster, a real one—anything would be better than this endless interlude, this tiresome life that never manages to rise to the dignity of a tragedy. (And we know that stress, which is indispensable for action, can, if excessive, lower resistance to disease.) "It's better to burn out than to fade away," said Neil Young, quoted by Kurt Cobain. However, even fading away is exorbitantly costly. There comes a time when the debt has to be paid, even if one has only wandered through dull and soporific terrains where an imperceptible corruption eats away at even the most shriveled destinies. That is why life is so endlessly short, so long it seems it will never end but always too short with respect to what is possible. We have a surplus of time that we start to miss as soon as it is past. The incoherent mumbling of our lives prevents us from making them works of art; in their density and unity, the latter transcend what defines us as human beings: incompletion, indetermination. The tedious sequence of passing days is anything but aesthetic, and no one can create himself like a painting, a sculpture, or a symphony. We are not masterpieces reflecting a perfect world, but artisans who have to shape themselves in a sinuous, unpredictable world.[3] In short, the labor of form is what separates life from art: it is form that condenses, purifies, orders, soothes our wounds by stylizing them, makes the tragic loveable and intolerable defeats bearable. (The only true happiness may be found in writing, life seeking after the fact to realize in itself the perfect junction of words, the coining of the precise expression.)

Everyday life thus allows us to believe in the coincidence of repetition and danger. The fewer things that happen, the more we seek to ensure that nothing happens. The simple anxiety of being gives rise to an irrepressible need for calm and relaxation. Hence the multitude of therapies under the aegis of Zen, Buddhism, Yoga; hence the abuse of vitamins, stimulants, tranquilizers, and other psychotropic drugs in America and Europe. Even if I lead the most stunted, lethargic life, I still have the feeling of being caught up in an unprecedented whirlwind that has to be slowed before I can do anything else. Trying to escape the busyness that arises from the emptiness of life by resorting to still more emptiness, that is the vicious circle that threatens us. Whereas in our colorless lives we need tranquility less than authentic activities, important and meaningful events, dazzling moments that prostrate us or transport us. Time, that great thief, is constantly stealing

---

[3] According to a distinction made by Pierre Aubenque between the Stoic sage and the Aristotelian sage: *La Prudence chez Aristote* (Paris: PUF, 1997), pp. 90, 91.

from us; but it is one thing to be robbed magnificently and to grow old in the awareness that one has lived a full and rich life, and it is another to be cheaply gnawed away, hour by hour, for things that we have not even known. Our contemporaries' hell is called platitude. The paradise they seek is called plenitude. Some have lived; the others have simply endured.

CHAPTER FIVE

The Extremists of Routine

My life began with extinction. It's odd, but that's
how it was. From my very first moments of
consciousness, I felt that I was dying.

—IVAN GONCHAROV, *Oblomov*

The Martyrs of the Dull

It is monastic life, with its meticulous division of the hours
of the day and its long periods reserved for prayer, that
best prefigures our present experience of profane time.
What is peculiar to a monk, if he belongs to a contempla-
tive order, is that he does nothing at all in the way of action or fabrication: he is subject, just as the rest of us are,
to the great disorganizing power that is called everyday
life, which can affect his faith and turn him away from
God. The spiritual exercises that each community has to
perform are intended to protect monks from dissipation
and to lead them to devote themselves entirely to the ado-
ration of God. It was probably in the hushed shadow of the
convents and monasteries that the West instilled in itself a
minute chronological discipline (later adopted by capitalism). A person who has fled the world to devote himself to

God lives in a framework regulated by the clock, of which the bells are the symbol. The monk is not a do-nothing or a parasite, as Luther and Calvin charged (replacing prayer with work, and making the latter virtually a religious act); he is, in a way, overworked. Like each of us, he is devoted to an essential and futile task: killing time, in this case, ordinary time, in order to gain eternity. When he is full of faith, every hour that he can give wholly to the glory of God is precious. But if he doubts or weakens, he is overcome by *acedia* (from the Greek *akedia*, indifference and despondency), that terrible malady of ascetics that turns them away from the Lord and makes them sorrowful. This is the fatigue of someone who has dedicated his life to prayer and whom prayer tires, who suffers from a sudden lack of interest in his salvation, a terrible problem that the Catholic Church has declared itself powerless to combat:

> when this has taken possession of some unhappy soul, it produces dislike of the place, disgust with the cell, and disdain and contempt of the brethren who dwell with him or at a little distance, as if they were careless or unspiritual. It also makes the man lazy and sluggish about all manner of work which has to be done within the enclosure of his dormitory. It does not suffer him to stay in his cell, or to take any pains about reading, and he often groans because he can do no good while he stays there.[1]

[1] St. John Cassian, *The Institutes of the Coenobia* (420 CE), book 10. See also Jean-Louis Chrétien's fine commentary in *De la fatigue* (Paris: Minuit, 1996), p. 92; and Jean Starobinski, "L'humeur et son changement," *Nouvelle Revue de psychanalyse* (Autumn 1985), p. 71.

In short, in these retreats where only fervor and contemplation should reign, boredom reintroduces moodiness, fog seeps in and corrupts the radiant house, attacks hearts, saps energies, and subjects the immutable to the assaults of the ephemeral. Lacking "the courage to endure duration" (V. Jankélévitch), the monk experiences a sort of internal rotting. Whence the necessity of keeping him busy night and day, taking control of his mental space, stopping the holes in his schedule, pestering him with various tasks that are as demanding as they are useless, for fear that the devil will sneak into him to hasten his slacking off. In his *Confessions*, St. Augustine recommends the practice of hymns and canticles to keep the "demoralized" from "drying up with boredom." Later on, St. Thomas blessed the obscurity of the Holy Scriptures, which forced the mind to make an effort of attention, and recommended prayers, neither too long nor too short, accompanied by an elaborate body language to spare believers the trouble of repressing yawns. Even God has a duty to be entertaining. The ascetic, the cenobite, and the hermit are historically the first martyrs of banality. Because their lives are reduced to a long invocation to the absent one, they are more exposed to the dangers of idleness and the miasmas of commonplace time. Let us avoid confusing everything by identifying monastic acedia with contemporary depression. Nonetheless, the recluse's torments prefigure boredom, the secular sin par excellence, which was already present in antiquity and which after the Renaissance became an ailment of the modern soul (whereas, with a few exceptions such as St. John Chrysostom, St. Gregory, and Christine de Pisan, it was rare in the Middle Ages).

The Emperor of Emptiness

One man embodies better than any other this fever of inanity: a little-known Swiss author named Henri-Frédéric Amiel (1821–1881), who wrote a diary sixteen thousand pages long, a monument to absolute emptiness, a frenetic copying down of the void, because each day is characterized by the fact that nothing happens. To judge by his diary, this great scholar, a professor at the University of Geneva, spent his time dreaming about the books he could have written and the women he did not marry. Perpetually incapable of making up his mind, in the grip of "the universal proteanism," he sought to remain backstage in life, only his diary, kept with meticulous care, giving him the illusion of having a destiny, an identity.[2] Other diarists may be more talented or famous, but Amiel is unique in his consistent focus on the tedious and repetitive.

Amiel interests us not only because of his vertiginous abulia but also because he takes the promotion of insignificance to previously unequaled heights. In this context, the insignificant is not what lacks meaning but what has not yet been given meaning. Amiel undertook to make something romantic and engaging out of nothing, an enterprise that is not without interest. His diary is a paper sanctuary dedicated to a new divinity: the infinitesimal, which he seeks to stage and throw light on. Moods, anecdotes, headaches, dyspepsia, respiratory problems,

[2] On Amiel, see Georges Poulet, *Études sur le temps humain* (Paris: Presses-Pocket, 2006), vol. 4, p. 266f., and Roland Jaccard, *Amiel, du journal intime* (Paris: Complexe, 1987).

all these little things end up making a story. A maniacal explorer of inwardness dedicated to the discontinuity of his impressions, "to the defects of microscopic analysis," he literally invented a new domain: the promotion of the trifle as an epic of the modern mind, of the accidental as a means of access to the essential. From each day he extracts his harvest of trinkets, awakening a whole inferior realm which his pen slowly brings into existence. And from this plainness he draws a paradoxical pride.

The less Amiel embraces the world, the more he has to write. The dreadful task of being absent from life and recording that absence, of being "a eunuch by vocation, a being without sex, vague and timorous," goes along with the observation that the daily is bottomless, limitless. The idea that every minute is full of an inexhaustible variety of thrills makes him dizzy, and this unexpectedly strengthens his mad, intense desire for sterility. If he castigates his work—"that forest of empty pages," that "scribbling reclusion"—he is even more dismayed to have failed to achieve his goal: what he brings together on paper each evening is still only a small part of what he has felt and observed. The strange fate of a penury that turns into a plethora. "These diaries are an illusion. They contain not even the tenth part of what I think in half an hour about something." "This diary is to the day what the pulp of a fruit is to its aroma. It collects the facts, the crude and ephemeral fiber of life, but the ethereal part, thoughts or feelings that have traversed the mind, evaporate without leaving a trace." A transmutation of the failure to live into an event, of a desert into a garden of Eden. His logorrhea is impotent, not because of a lack, but because of an excess of material. This interminable soliloquy dedicated to the goddess of infertility sins by falling short: his problem is not that he says too much but that he does not say enough. This colossal encyclopedia of nothingness is still a slender volume in comparison to those that he should fill.

Then what is the point of living if this narrow stream already overwhelms him by its profusion? (And modernity is full of these heroes of extinction and quasi-death who, like Oblomov, display an exceptional inertia, raising lethargy and indolence to the level of absolute values.) Amiel's embryonic life, reduced to its simplest expression, is still an irrepressible torrent, and his words proliferate without any need for confirmation by the facts. A singular reversal: the author no longer writes to recount what he has experienced, but to persuade himself that he is alive, to amplify himself, even if in the realm of the minimal and the infinitesimal; he is dazzled by the inexhaustible wealth concealed by a fate apparently so mediocre. And his *journal intime*, or rather his *journal de l'infime*, thus creates its own reader, a brother in banality, who takes pleasure in seeing the author storing away, week after week, his pathetic harvests. I am an abyss—Amiel tells us—and every year I experience 365 different fates (the day as a total human drama: Joyce and Woolf made that a great theme of the twentieth-century novel). One might think our Swiss professor was tired of living. But Amiel was hyperactive, drawing on great resources of energy to ensure that nothing happened to him. There are no limits to inconsistency: that is what he discovered with terror when he plunged into the vertiginous microcosm of his lifelessness.

Amiel may have inaugurated a new form of happiness, nonlife as ascesis, a neurosis peculiar to modernity, the contrary of Romantic hysteria. An empty destiny, a desperate drivel, so boring that it takes on a fantastic dimension. Whereas a hero is a person who lives in a constant state of emergency and moves directly from one exploit to the next, Amiel knows nothing but moments of inactivity surrounded by long periods of emptiness. It is as if he had chosen to reside in limbo, the prince of a ridiculous kingdom called abstention, lack of achievement. An extraordinary life in its own way, built on a permanent hemorrhage and resembling a secular mysticism of annihilation. Our own time is full of these extremists of routine who force themselves to endure a salutary blandness: for instance, the participants in a strange rite, the "Congrès de Banalyse," which takes place every year in a former railway station in France, or the Dutch artist who took a vow of noninformation and launched in April 1998 a magazine consisting of sixteen blank pages, to appear irregularly, in order to leave the reader royally in peace. Whereas social life speeds on and imposes its pace, these deserters slow down and espouse everyday apathy with such enthusiasm that they throw it off the rails, beat it at its own game. There are ultimately two ways of escaping banality: either by fleeing it or by embracing it so tightly that one sabotages it from within.

The Utopia of Fun

A distant descendant of British self-composure and a near cousin of "cool," fun does not imply a morality of amusement, and still less a morality of the *dérèglement de tous les sens* such as was urged by Rimbaud. On the contrary, it constitutes a system of selection that makes it possible to isolate within ordinary life a pure core of pleasure that is neither too strong nor too weak, that has no negative consequences, and that takes us into a universe of agreeable sensations. Anything can become fun, that is, the object of a light effervescence—sex or chastity, marriage or travel, religion or political commitment—provided that one does not pursue the latter too far. Fun is therefore a discipline of sifting that erects subtle ramparts, creates an aseptic environment in which I take pleasure in the world without giving it the right to wound or punish me in return. A discreet dissidence that rejects the hysteria of an intense life as well as that of bustling activity and conceives only of a filtered entertainment, once a protective cushion has been placed between us and things to protect us from bitterness and harshness.

In this respect, fun is contemporary with the virtual and like it testifies to the same will to dematerialize the world, to shake up the boundaries between space and time. A little of this dimension is found in sports like surfing, which embraces waves the better to play with them; Rollerblading, which transforms asphalt into a long, smooth ribbon along which sail shadowy figures of prodigious elegance weaving among pedestrians and laughing at obstacles; free-ride snowboarding, which makes the snowboarder a bird that can dance in the air, fly over rocky ridges, and caress the powder. The miracle of all these feats is that they efface the body by means of the body, they attain weightlessness. A universe of spirits and elves who can walk through walls, for whom the laws of gravity no longer exist, and who fluidify matter. You have to be weightless, you have to soar. The human dream of being disengaged and unencumbered, which privileges sensation over experience, skimming over being rooted. The real in all its density is called upon only the better to elude it. And just as we can now sing a duet with Elvis or play in a Bogart film, thanks to virtual technologies, so fun thrusts us into the enchantment of fairy tales: desire overcomes all obstacles and easily achieves full satisfaction. The universe has lost its asperity; it has been reduced to a surface, to forms, to images. So we can try everything, on the condition that nothing has any importance. That is what fun is: a utopia in which all burdens are lifted, all pleasures are allowed, and all misfortunes are dodged. With fun, life becomes a game for which there is no price to be paid.

The Passion for Weather

Amiel was not only the first to go all the way in pursuing nullity and dream of resigning from the world, he also invented (after Rousseau and Maine de Biran) something that was to become a leitmotif of his century and the following ones: weather in its relations to our moods. Others before him had studied the influence of climate on political systems or described the mind as an atmospheric substance whose variations could be measured.[3] Amiel systematized

---

[3] See Pierre Pachet, *Les Baromètres de l'âme* (Paris: Hatier, 1990), pp. 37–38.

this kind of notation. Every entry in his diary begins with a comment on the weather made as if he had to consult the skies to know how he felt: "Bright sun, as joyous as yesterday"; "Gray and overcast, the heat wave seems to be over"; "Gray sky, cold, dreary, not a ray of sun, without love, it corresponds to the disenchanted life of someone who has not dared offer his hand to a woman and say: Under God's protection, will you cross over with me and bind yourself to me by an oath? The sky is bearable but reminds me of the color of the cloister and that of renunciation"; "A fine sun is flooding into my bedroom, nature is celebrating, autumn smiling. I respond to these advances as best I can."[4]

Meteorology emerged as a democratic passion at the turn of the nineteenth century when, ceasing to be only a predictive science that was initially useful to farmers and sailors, it became a science of the inner life, that is, of moods. What is a mood but a relationship between the world and us that brings into conjunction wavering beings and a constantly changing nature? By accustoming us to the attractions of the irregular, to small variations, meteorology teaches us about minuscule diversity: if nothing happens to us, at least it rains, the wind blows, the sun shines. The charm of today's weather is its instability, and instability is also the charm of changing weather, of its constantly shifting kaleidoscope. By making our senses and perception more acute, the weather shapes an ethics of the in-between, of half-tones, of nuance. And since the passing of the seasons is enough for the feeling

---

[4] Quotations taken from vol. 12 of Amiel's *Journal* (Geneva: L'Âge d'Homme, 1994).

of existence, it revives the Greek idea of the cosmos, of a solidarity between the elements and the human heart, a communion for which we are all nostalgic.

In his *Pensées*, Pascal wrote: "The weather and my mood have little connection. I have my foggy and my fine days within me; my prosperity or misfortune has little to do with the matter." The believer, whose faith is unshakable, does not suffer from modern sensitivities that are alarmed by bad weather or delighted by a ray of sunshine. Weather is naturally contemporaneous with the global village, and it now includes the ups and downs of the stock market, currency exchange rates, and raw materials prices. Permanently visible in a corner of the screen, the stock market index, rising and falling from minute to minute, is analogous to the Roman emperor's thumb that spared or doomed gladiators. Because it connects outer and inner conditions, since the 1950s weather has become a hedonic symbol for Western nations. Weather channels on television have to be both precise and euphoric. A perturbation is preferably brief and precedes an improvement, sunny weather preferably accompanies vacationers but does not degenerate into a heat wave or drought. Ideal weather is both constant and moderate. Thus the weatherman pulls a long face when forecasting a cold and rainy period—then he is the bearer of bad news, and even its accomplice—but he cheers up when good weather returns. In every case he has to combine the gravity of a scientist with the solicitude of a mother as he tells us: "If you go to Warsaw tonight, don't forget to take your overcoat! Those of you going on to Moscow better take a heavy sweater along, too."

Since the weather is the *skin of the world*, our primor-
dial garment, it guarantees my life, in a way, and tells me
how I must be. That is why Roland Barthes said that the
weather is the most serious subject of conversation there
is. We know that certain nervous systems register the nu-
ances of the atmosphere with an almost electric sensitivity,
making of the slightest hint of mist or haziness a whole exhausting drama (since 1987, seasonal affective disorder, or
SAD, has been listed as a type of cyclical depression in the
Diagnostic and Statistical Manual of Mental Disorders[5]).
Our bodies are imbued by a great cosmic body that draws
us into its tremors, its sighs, its tempests; we suffer from its
illnesses as much as we benefit from its upturns. Sunlight
fills us with a feeling of elation, dilates our souls as far as
the confines of the universe, just as a gray, heavy sky con-
tracts our hearts. What is most distant is closest, and turbulent weather is a personal tragedy.

However, the correlation between inside and outside is
invalidated almost as soon as it is postulated. Meteorology
is less a science than a propitiatory rite, a technical variant of prophecy like horoscopes and numerology, but
with a higher degree of plausibility. Through its predictions, an unpredictable divinity honors us or punishes us
for our sins, the gravest of which are the excesses of industrial societies, which are punished by tornados, tidal
waves, and hurricanes (to which male and female names
are given in alternation, so as not to offend either sex). In

[5] This work, usually known as the DSM, is a standard manual published
by the American Psychiatric Association. Cited in Martin de la Soudière, *Au
bonheur des saisons* (Paris: Grasset, 1999), p. 272.

the United States there are bold surfers who wait at the eye of the storm for the ultimate wave that will carry them to another world (like the mythical photographer who, it is said, was at the eye of Hurricane Andrew, which ravaged the Bahamas and South Florida in August 1992. He is supposed to have survived but gone insane). We feel a mixture of horror and jubilation when a blizzard or tornado pulverizes the usual weather, dramatizes the everyday, and transports us into the sublime, that is, into a dimension of superhuman grandeur. These are upheavals that affect us all, even if nothing happens to us as individuals. In its banality the weather conceals an element of pagan sacredness; it is our last supernatural phenomenon (in the early 1980s Pope John Paul II went to pray in southern Italy in order to end a drought there). That is why weather is one of our great consolations. It is, however, an uncertain consolation because it can be neither controlled nor directed. Thus the gestures and supplications we make to the enigmatic spirits on high, those changeable deities who decide our fate and whose countless caprices we call showers, hail, cold, hurricanes, winds, floods—all ways of torturing us poor humans.

In the end, we are no more masters of the weather than we are masters of ourselves, and we decipher the skies with the same perplexity as we do the movements of our hearts. As for the supposed analogy between the atmosphere and our moods, it is far from clear: the luxuriance of brilliant sunshine can hurt us, gray clouds can make us happy, and snow and cold can elicit a long-lasting delight. The weather is an aleatory oracle. It combines two contradictory ideas of happiness, the happiness of being one with the world and that of thwarting the world. On the one hand, the osmosis between humans and the universe is fragile: the secret rotation of our inner seasons is not always linked to the elements. On the other hand, we tend to free ourselves from the order of the seasons while at the same time suffering from their slightest rigors as if they were insulting our will to autonomy. We are scandalized that it is hot in summer and that it snows in winter: we behave with regard to the weather like spoiled children who want to summon it or send it away as we see fit (in 1986, on a particularly cold day in January, staff members of the French satirical review *Jalons* marched through Paris chanting, "Winter's too cold, Mitterrand's to blame").

If landslides, avalanches, and floods now result in lawsuits, that is because for us there are no longer any natural catastrophes, only cases of human negligence. Whenever a tragedy occurs, we have to find someone who is responsible for it. We have moved from fatalism to penalism; we are distressed less than we are inclined to blame, especially at a time when scapegoats are readily available. Since we have claimed to shape and master nature, it is only normal that we become accountable for nature's turmoil. But the enormous power that we are thereby given surprises and crushes us. We may sue the national weather service for issuing erroneous predictions, and we may soon sue Mother Nature because of her bad character, her calamitous shivers, and her evil exhalations. But when a genuine disaster strikes Europe, our first reaction is to be stunned and at a loss because we are unprepared for extreme situations (unlike the United States), because we have done away with the very idea of risk and bad weather. Thus there is a twofold will to embrace the world and to free ourselves from it: dependency devastates and humiliates us, but total independence distresses us just as much because it isolates us. On the one hand, we need communion, and on the other, self-affirmation, and modern consciousness, halfway between its dream of mastery and its dream of harmony, cannot choose between the two.

The Adventures of the Sick Body

What has happened to you in your life? Many people might reply: I've had ulcers, a heart attack, rheumatism. . . . My body has told stories that I can spin out in the form of little narratives that sum up my biography. Falling ill gives you something to say about yourself that goes beyond the ordinary, a way of attracting attention. What is an illness, after all? A transformation of the organism that can be an experience and not merely an upheaval. Here we are not talking about romanticizing pain or the outdated myth that saw the origin of every great work in some recurrent disease—asthma in Proust, epilepsy in Dostoyevsky, syphilis in Baudelaire—that led Drieu La Rochelle to write: "People in good health are dull exemplars." Of course, everyone avoids illness and the terrible torments it can produce are undeniable. But it cannot be seen solely as a diminished state of being, a subtraction,[6] a mere alternation of fevers and symptoms: it is also a life event. If despite my best efforts I fall ill, I can always take over my illness, appropriate it, adapt to my own ends this foreignness that has risen from my body. Even faced with the most atrocious suffering, I still can make use of language, of the sovereign freedom to recount my suffering and thus keep it at a distance.

The ups and downs of the ailing body (these are the corollary of the ecstasies of the erotic body: pleasure is expanding just as pain is enclosing) testify to a life engaged solely in rumination and concerned only with itself. There is nothing sadder than listening to old men in a rest home talking endlessly about their prostates, their lungs, or their kidneys, obsessed by the drivel of their organs, by the saga of an obstructed bladder, swollen feet, and clogged veins. We toss our little problems into the common pot, try to tell the most horrible story; our ordeals create bonds, forge ephemeral tribes of diabetics, heart patients, headache sufferers. That is what extreme old age is: the time when all one's energy goes into self-preservation, when hanging on has become so difficult that every day is a victory over collapse. The slow and silent extinction of a life

---

[6] Georges Canguilhem has argued that sickness constitutes a new dimension of life, the living person's positive experience of something new that retains the ability to be normative. See his *Le Normal et la Pathologique* (Paris: PUF, 1991), pp. 122–123. On the other hand, François Dagognet shows how much sickness is another aspect of life of which everyone is both the victim and the beneficiary: "When one chooses his life, he chooses his illness." *Pour une philosophie de la maladie* (Paris: Textuel, 1996).

that is flickering out and is reduced to a few essential functions: eating, drinking, sleeping, dragging oneself along and trying to keep things going; beyond a certain point, time undoes us more than it makes us, and the losses are irreversible.

Thus there are two ways of breathing excitement into life when nothing is happening to us: listening to one's mind and relating one's physiological sufferings. By inventing the unconscious, Freudianism gave a new impetus to the art of introspection. Thanks to this inexhaustible echo chamber, every life is endowed with an unexpected depth. The result is an unprecedented increase in commentary: just as dreams are the profusion of plots that the brain offers us when we are simply sleeping, our most benign behaviors have a meaning: slips and mistakes transform the dullest lives into tumultuous stampedes. Everyone can talk about himself, rummage around in his psychic cellars and bring back a supply of fables and enigmas that create a kind of embellishment of the ordinary. There are no longer any insignificant individuals, only great ones who are not yet aware of themselves but who have the psychic opulence of a Michelangelo, a Borgia, or a Shakespeare.

Similarly, sickness can become a way of life, a means for converting everyday life into fiction or even a criminal investigation, because our body shelters a potential killer, its own death. By tearing us away from the obviousness of the everyday, it dramatizes mechanical gestures and gives them an extreme density. In sickness, the anodyne coincides with the dangerous, and a trifle can be the prelude to a general disorder (many serious illnesses establish themselves in us without warning). The hypochondriac's tragicomedy consists in madly anticipating his own decline, seeing a headache or a cramp in his arm as a death sentence, and then actually falling ill someday, thus confirming his darkest diagnoses. With certain ailments, we enter into a high-risk universe. And for someone who is hanging on only by adhering to an austere diet, a glass of wine, a pinch of salt, a pat of butter can become the equivalent of Russian roulette. Every patient experiences, as a result of his illness, a paradoxical intensification of his existence, which is transformed into a road with multiple ambushes, especially when every deviation comes at a high price. Nothing in the body can be taken for granted, every part can deteriorate, every organ can torture us, life can kill life: that is what we realize during moments of physical exhaustion (according to the World Health Organization, there are more than forty thousand diseases, forty thousand ways of being dismissed from this world, without counting combinations and complications).

Every assault on our physical integrity is punctuated by crises and remissions. Passions may dwindle during these assaults, but this dwindling is full of minuscule expectations, little surprises. Thus we see patients sometimes preferring their current condition to a hypothetical recovery that would return them to the common lot. Like Svevo's Zeno, who, delighted that he is not regaining his health, venerates his organic failings as if they were treasures:

Sickness is a conviction, and I was born with that conviction.... Diabetes was, I admit, a great pleasure for me. . . . I cherished my disease. I recalled with sympathy poor Copler, who preferred real illness to imaginary illness. I agreed with him. Sickness is very simple: all you have to do is let yourself be carried along. In fact, when I read the description of a diabetic in a medical manual I found in it a whole program for living, not for dying, for living. Farewell resolutions, farewell projects! Henceforth I no longer had to do anything: I was free![7]

Not only does being sick confer a personality on an individual—classical suffering was the common lot of all, whereas modern suffering is an identity and almost a reason for being—but sickness can be the subject of a narrative, especially when it has been overcome. And if some people choose to ignore it, others brandish it like a talisman to elicit mercy, to tyrannize those around them, or simply to make themselves interesting.[8] In this respect, everyone navigates among three reefs that are almost three narrative constraints: suffering from a benign disease that is not worth mentioning (for example, flu, which puts you in bed but whose yield in terms of compassion is zero because it is so common), a chronic illness that is boring because it goes on and on, and a disease so terrible that it is repellent. And one may wish to be sick in order to experience the marvelous pleasure of recovering, skirting the abyss in order to draw back from it. A euphoric moment when

[7] Italo Svevo, *The Confessions of Zeno*, trans. Beryl de Zoete (New York: New Directions, 1930).

[8] On the refusal to recover because of the gratifications provided by being sick, see Édouard Zarifian, *La Force de guérir* (Paris: Odile Jacob, 1999).

an infection subsides, giving you back your strength and the use of your body: exhaustion has the ability to make ordinary well-being seem marvelous and the first days of convalescence seem so desirable. We return from illness like glorious conquerors, and sicknesses are the battles of the modern citizen, on which he reports the way soldiers used to tell tales of their campaigns. Some people invent terrible wounds the way others invent terrible sins to tell their confessors, in order to make themselves special.

A Delicious Terror

Edgar Allan Poe remarked that fear is a feeling that people like to have when they are sure they are safe. The advent of banality in the West seems to have given us two new literary categories, the detective novel and fantastic literature. These emerged when the era of miracles peculiar to the Middle Ages came to an end, as a way of breaking out of a universe deprived of magic and the gods and already disciplined by work, science, and technology. That is why horror books and films function to infect a space that was magical in fairy tales but is now poisoned. The ordinary becomes terrifying, full of occult powers and palpable threats.

Nevertheless, we must distinguish the classical detective novel, which narrates the irruption and elimination of disorder within civilized society, from the hard-boiled crime story, which follows the course of a wholly chaotic world in which justice and clarity no longer exist. In this respect American culture has invented two new genres: the Western, which precedes the law, and the thriller, which is outside or alongside the law. The savagery of a humanity at the frontiers of civilization, on the one hand,

and the barbarity of an urban jungle and the dark corners of society, on the other.

In the fantastic as in the detective novel, we get thrills without harmful consequences, without risks. Comfortably settled into our easy chairs, we take delight in reassuring abominations: the pleasure of recognition and being on familiar ground. This cult of the atrocious is first of all a cult for stay-at-homes. We agree to tremble with fear only because we know we are safe; we succumb to the comfort of terror, and this controlled terror keeps in check those that usually assail us. Scaring ourselves to tame our fear, that is the pleasure of the hard-boiled crime novel, the horror film.

There is at least this much that is positive about these morbid fictions: unlike our current mythologies, they conceal neither evil nor death, and that is why they so often have religious connotations. In times of calm, we need to look horror in the face, to know what is going on behind the excessively tranquil stage-setting of our lives. We need everyday rites to help us live in close proximity to disaster.

But when he returns to ordinary life, the spectator or reader remains haunted by all the fears that have emerged on the screen or between the pages and that he has temporarily exorcised. They accompany him, tug at his sleeve, whisper to him that they might actually strike him in the real world. The artist's domestication of the terrifying by artistic means is fragile: it is in full daylight that curses sprout and monsters and killers proliferate. Then we have to go back to darkened theaters, plunge back into another diabolical plot, inject ourselves with another dose of fear at regular intervals in order to conjure all the evil powers that swarm in the interstices of comfort and passivity.

Joy, Spinoza wrote, is knowing that something hateful has been destroyed, speaking about a danger one has escaped. As if the fact of having run a risk and having survived immediately made you part of an aristocracy, endowed you with the heroic virtue par excellence (especially in the Mediterranean basin), *bàraka* (a combination of courage and luck). There is nothing our societies admire more than a survivor, whether he has emerged safe and sound from an accident, cancer, or a coma, and especially when science has already said his case was hopeless.

Whether we fight them or succumb to them, sicknesses give us a history. Some of them marginalize us, while others project us into a clandestine society with its own rites and traditions. In any case, they testify to our ability to shape misfortune if we cannot rid ourselves of it, to convert our weaknesses into creative experiences. Even injured, life can still give rise to a world, display itself, dramatize its own infirmities. This small achievement itself still constitutes a cosmos.

CHAPTER SIX

Real Life Is Not Absent

I believe more in death in life than in life after death.

—ANDRÉ GREEN

What can you do if you are thirty and, turning
the corner of your own street, you are overcome,
suddenly by a feeling of bliss—absolute bliss!—as
though you'd suddenly swallowed a bright piece of
that late afternoon sun and it burned in your bosom,
sending out a little shower of sparks into every
particle, into every finger and toe? . . .

—KATHERINE MANSFIELD

Joy is the passage of man from a lesser perfection
to a greater. Sorrow is the passage of man from a
greater perfection to a lesser.

—SPINOZA

Missed Appointments with Destiny

A man and a woman meet by chance at the home of friends
ten years after they first met. From his earliest childhood,
the man, John Marcher, has had "the sense of being kept for

something rare and strange, possibly prodigious and terrible, that was sooner or later to happen" to him. This unforesee-able thing awaited him "amid the twists and the turns of the months and the years, like a crouching beast in the Jungle."[1] It will spring on him at some time or another, he just has to be prepared. He asks the young woman, May Bartram, to wait with him for this extraordinary event. Being one of the elect, he is not afraid to melt into ordinary humanity, for the secret he bears within him makes him unlike anyone else.

The years pass by, the man and woman grow old together, always on their guard. One day the "admirable friend" falls ill. Before she dies, she tells the man, "You've nothing to wait for more. It has come." In the cemetery where she is buried, Marcher happens to meet a young man ravaged by the recent loss of his wife; inexplicably, Marcher envies the man's sorrow, "the glare of his grief." "What had the man *had*, to make him by the loss of it so bleed and yet live?" Suddenly Marcher realizes that the beast in the jungle had May Bartram's face and that he has missed it. "The escape would have been to love her; then, *then* he would have lived."[2] Sharing the affection she had for him, he would finally have known a passion that would devastate him and allow him to experience the savor of life. But walled up in his obsession, he remained someone "to whom nothing will ever happen."

A splendid fable: the worst thing that can happen is in fact to encounter our happiness and not recognize it. To wait for a miraculous event in the hope that it will someday

---

[1] "The Beast in the Jungle," in *The Portable Henry James* (New York: Viking, 1951), pp. 279, 286.
[2] Ibid., pp. 324, 325.

redeem us and fail to see that the miracle resides in the event that we are experiencing. To believe that our lives are for the moment a simple sketch that will soon turn into something more intense: a permanent postponement of pleasure that strangely resembles religious asceticism. As if a prehistory composed of trivialities were supposed to be followed by a transfiguration, a definitive farewell to all human miseries.

Missed opportunities: a word unspoken, a hand not extended, a gesture begun and then retracted—these are moments when out of fear or timidity our fate does not change. Too soon, too late: there are lives that remain wholly doomed to the unfulfilled, the unaccomplished. What might have been, what was not: some people are satisfied with this conditional, and we all could write the story of the destinies we have avoided and that accompany us like so many phantasmal possibilities. Brassaï tells how, at the age of twenty-two, Marcel Proust became infatuated with a young man, the son of a Genevan magistrate. On the back of the photograph the young man gave Proust was written the following dedication taken from a sonnet by the Pre-Raphaelite painter Dante Gabriel Rossetti: "Look at my face; my name is Might-have-been; I am also called No-more, Too-late, Farewell."[3] Every life being unique, it rejects and excludes others. Or else it builds itself upon a crime: that of the virtualities it has killed and that have not been able to develop. It does not help to know that every instant provides possible new departures, that it is not too late

---

[3] Anecdote reported by Roland Jaccard, *Le Monde*, October 24, 1997.

until the last breath is drawn, the event is decisive: whatever takes place erases other potentialities. And for those who are not granted a second chance, possibilities then begin to run short. People stop holding out their hands; the road stops bifurcating and remains hopelessly straight and flat.

Another, more beautiful, more ardent life exists! What child or adolescent, stagnating in some monotone family, has not heard this call with a shiver of pleasure? No one is doomed to remain in the condition into which he was born, in his social, parental, or conjugal situation. The mere premonition of a more favorable destiny often suffices to tear down the walls that imprison us. That is the charm of departing and breaking away: they cast us into the unknown and make a beneficial rip in the fabric of time. To the principles of pleasure and reality we should add a third: the principle of exteriority, insofar as it is the realm of the diversity and inexhaustible savor of things. Life also proceeds by revelations when we are suddenly offered an intuition of other, upsetting worlds, as when Flaubert's Pécuchet is galvanized by the sexual frolics of a splendidly indecent peasant girl he observes behind a hedge. We have to leave a door open to "the country outside" (Lewis Carroll), to mystery, the unexplored, and at least once we have to go through this door, respond to the call of other places—for some, the desert, Asia, or Africa, for others the discovery of a new sexuality, a stifled vocation. Then everything hangs on the imminence of an evasion, a leap that will deliver us from the asphyxiating powers of routine and pettiness. A luminous moment of narrow escape that carries us toward happier shores.

But if we can put our lives at stake as if we were casting a die, sail off toward new destinies, it is not true that we can do whatever we want, be anyone at all, slip into the skins of a scholar, artist, astronaut, one after the other, and that "the sky's the limit." That is the American attitude of "can do" that sets no limit to an individual's capacities provided that he roll up his sleeves, the optimism of a pioneer nation that believes in the marriage of efficacy and will. The Old Regime's constraint of salvation has given way in secular societies to the intoxication with a range of possibilities so wide that it makes one giddy. Someone who hopes to embrace every possibility is likely to fully embrace none; it is one thing to move beyond oneself, and another to think one doesn't have to make choices, that is, that one can escape a framework which, by restraining us, is also the condition of our freedom.

This may be the paradox: the quest for a good life has to obey two contradictory commands: take full advantage of what comes along, but also remain alert to what is happening elsewhere. A near-sighted wisdom immersed in the present, satisfied to be what it is, and a far-sighted wisdom that makes plans and is never satisfied with its condition. On the one hand, the philosophy of carpe diem that asks us to consider every day as if it were our last, and on the other hand a hope for something better, a rejection of a happiness forced upon us (by the family, the social order) in the name of a desired happiness. A contraction that seals us up inside ourselves or an expansion that dilates us to the dimensions of the universe (that was the schema that opposed Rousseau to Diderot), serenity or restlessness, autarky or drunkenness—we seldom escape these dilemmas.

So there are two kinds of possibility: a crushing possibility that devours reality from the heights of its majesty and sees everything we experience as meager and inadequate (that is the disease from which James's Marcher suffers). And an enriching possibility that brings to light everything that lies dormant in people. *A possibility-sarcophagus or a possibility-chrysalis*: one is the bearer of such amplitude that it sterilizes my slightest initiatives and makes me despair of undertaking anything, the other points toward a richer time that is both a rupture and a continuity and concerns "what it is sweet to imagine," as Kant said about utopia. In one case life succumbs under the weight of the unlimited, in the other it liberates all its latencies as the sun actualizes and awakens all colors.

The Poison of Envy

Contrary to official optimism, there is nothing we find more intolerable than the sight of someone else's happiness when things are not going well for us. The spectacle of these people parading about, rewarded a hundred times over with fortune's gifts, with health and with love, the ostentatious way they strut and thrust out their chests, that is what we find odious! That is why the daily contemplation of the world's horrors on the television news can have a calming effect: it is not that we take particular pleasure in seeing other people's misfortunes, but they allow us to feel ourselves less alone and even lucky: "Pleasant it is, when over a great sea the winds trouble the waters, to gaze from shore upon another's great tribulation" (Lucretius). This is consolation by comparison: we need other people's disasters to help us endure our own and to see that there is always something worse elsewhere, that our condition is not so cruel after all. Bitterness generally arises from the contrast between my fate and that of others who are better off and begins an endless chain of dissatisfactions. "To be poor in Paris is to be poor twice over," Zola said, so much does the proximity of wealth drive the poor mad. And the French literary and intellectual environment could be analyzed from the three points of view of disappointment, meanness, and calumny. How many quenchless hatreds, how many thunderous quarrels were first motivated by bitterness and jealousy and then concealed under political or philosophical garments?

Because they are egalitarian, our democratic societies are envious and encourage anger at the slightest privilege accorded someone else (especially in the particularly intolerable form of privilege known as luck). We can envy a face, a physical detail, a brand of car, a lover; we can even envy someone else's misery or illnesses when we find them more chic than our dull condition. We must not overwhelm others with our misfortunes any more than we must crush them with the splendors of our success. This involves a subtle calculation that leads us to avoid mentioning good news, to dress modestly, pull a long face, in short, to convert discretion into a strategy for achieving distinction. Similarly, we have to pretend to disdain those who are better off than we in order to protect ourselves from being eaten away by rancor.

Envy has another, deeper source: the more happiness establishes itself as a universal goal, the more it is emptied of content. The vagueness of its message constitutes both its strength and its curse: that is why we can sincerely pity all those who invest an inordinate amount of energy in building up this enigmatic treasure and who think they have failed if they do not achieve it immediately. (But if happiness eludes those who seek it, that does not mean that it favors those who flee it.) No one is ever sure that he is truly happy; and to ask the question is already to spoil the answer. Just as for Calvinists there were no certain criteria that allowed one to know whether one was among the elect or the damned, we base our feeling that we are happy solely on our inner conviction. But it is a conviction that the presence of others can dissipate in a moment: I thought I was the happiest of men and now, in the course of a conversation, I learn that a friend's vacation was more exciting than mine, that he has a more varied love life or more attractive professional prospects. Conclusion: I'm just a poor wretch hooked up to a mediocre fate.

In short, the competition of desires can plunge us into perpetual torment. No matter how high our position, it cannot protect us from animosity directed against someone in a higher position. And we refuse to really live anything because somewhere others are living better. Then we transform our happiness into a status, *we display our titles of felicity the way others display their titles of nobility.* The point is not to be happy but to know that others are unhappy and are mortified about it. One of Racine's characters puts it well: "A happiness so common has no attraction for me. It isn't happiness if it doesn't make people envious." But in addition to the fact that we think others are more well-adjusted or depressed than they are, this is a miserable triumph because it brings with it all the problems that it wanted to avoid. The struggle is endless when it bears on trivial details, and nothing can pacify a vanity that constantly spoils our peace and transforms itself into an all-devouring concern.

How can we escape this vicious circle that hurls us from rage to disarray? We surely miss happiness by thinking that it is not the right one, to which only the rare elect hold the key. But matters would be simpler if we could be satisfied with the happiness we have. What makes most discussions of happiness so insipid is that they deliver one and the same message: accept your fate, moderate your desires, want what you have and you'll have what you want. Wise counsel that is as resigned as it is trite, amalgamating all sorts of spiritualities, celebrity magazines, and official comforters. A sad dream of eternal respite! If there is a danger in going astray along the paths to conventional beatitude, in embracing professional, conjugal, or family life in the certainty that it will bring us the rapture we so much desire, we also deprive ourselves of the best things the world has to offer by ignoring or scorning the examples provided by others. Others are not simply rivals, censors, or judges: they are also prompters, in the sense this word has taken on in the theater. They "prompt" us, suggesting countless other ways of living, of blazing new paths. The venomous vapors of envy can then be turned into emulation, into curiosity, the Other becoming a guide for our desires rather than an intolerable obstacle to them. There are many other roads to joy in this world, other forms of contentment. Just as a work of art reveals new aspects of life to us and thus helps embellish it, there are Sirens around us, solar, radiant beings who invite us to try on other destinies. They are the ones who experiment with new arts of living, wrench happiness away from its canonical definitions, and set it upon new avenues. It is sometimes good to yield to their call, to follow them the way children follow the Pied Piper because they instill "new vices" in us (André Breton). Nothing would be sadder than to stubbornly miss out on one's own time, on what is best in its madness, its inventions. This leads to a double impasse: being caught like a chameleon by all the authorized images of felicity or remaining walled up in oneself, ruminating on one's little life as if it were flavorless chewing gum. Joy is contagious, irresistibly attractive. One may prefer to the company of the hypocrites who circle greedily around misfortune that of passionate people, bons vivants whose sole presence is a promise of expansion and gaiety.

The Mystique of Culminations

In late 1998 the London *Times* published a moving and revealing story about a certain Andrew Park, who decided in 1993 to celebrate Christmas every day. He did not fail to do so even once, winter or summer. Every evening he put three gifts in his slippers at the base of a decorated Christmas tree and opened them the next morning with astonishment. But Christmas every day ended up weighing on him: turkey, sherry, chocolate, and pudding, evening after evening led to budgetary problems and a diet that was both too rich and too monotonous. The ceremonial turned into a nightmare. "I need help," Park said. "I like having Christmas every day. But I know that it's becoming dangerous."[4]

Do away with everyday life! Who has not dreamed of this at one time or another? In its most radical forms, this utopia was realized in twentieth-century totalitarian states that succeeded in destroying the status quo in the name of a mystique of movement and aggressiveness. For the time being, we have not found a better remedy for the terrible banality of life than to throw ourselves into terror and war. Without going to these extremes, the refusal to come to terms "with the ridiculous conditions of all life in the world" (André Breton) can lead to a powerful desire to break the dikes, to step outside ordinary respectability. Balzac praised people whose life is no more than a series of poems in action and who "make novels rather than writing them." In *L'Histoire des Treize*, he recounted the exploits of exceptional individuals, survivors of the Napoleonic Empire, all of whom were motivated by the cult of energy, a rejection of platitudes, and the frenzy of pleasure. Should we adopt that alternative? Is our only choice between excess and stinginess?

As we have seen, the great utopian dream of the 1960s was to decree perpetual pleasure, a permanent state of happiness.

[4] Quoted by Pierre Georges, *Le Monde*, December 16, 1998.

Then it was a matter of crystallizing the chaotic flow of days into a single moment of sublime fervor, immersing the everyday in effervescence. A magnificent and terrible utopia, of which the situationists were the main standard-bearers. But by repeating over and over that "people live in a state of creativity twenty-four hours a day" (Raoul Vaneigem), the enemies of boredom transplanted into the order of pleasure a productivist logic that replicates that of the industrial system. In both cases, everything has to be maximized, subjected to the imperative of profitability. Neither pleasure nor production can tolerate the slightest pause. In that very way the partisans of intensity show the same animosity toward this imperfect existence as Christians used to show toward the human condition. For them as for Bossuet, ordinary life is the sin par excellence, abomination itself. Humans always have to be reprimanded, made ashamed to be only what they are. What the far Left and the extreme Right have rehabilitated in their aversion to bourgeois society is simply the idea of original sin: *life is fundamentally guilty of being everyday*, and anyone who endorses it is an accomplice in the supreme crime. (The situationists' convulsive prophecies required no demonstration or verification and gave rise to fine phrases and furious, lapidary remarks, but also to a vast treasury of sententious ineptitudes of which someone like Guy Debord, now beatified and embalmed in the wax museum of subversion, made immoderate use.)

Erected into an absolute, intensity became so intransigent that it turned into a slander on life. If pleasure is the sole reality, it merges with the order of things and thus is no longer pleasure (which is shown at another level by prostitution, which makes the most intense act, sexual intercourse, mechanical and commercial). There comes a time when all these expressions used mechanically— "passion," "desire," "pleasure," "the sovereign will to life"— turn into a kind of mumbo jumbo, mere jingles: pleasure cures have gone the way of the market or the revolution, and their advocates are no less driveling. But above all we need "down days" in life, *we have to preserve at all costs unequal densities in life*, if only for the pleasure of contrast. Great surges of elation usually occur against a background of expectations and trivial concerns that they illuminate and from which they distinguish themselves. A burst of joy lights up a day that was previously neither good nor bad and lends it color. Although there are days that detach themselves from time and allow us to experience a kind of eternity, we cannot rely on them to inaugurate an era of perfection; from the height of a splendid instant we fall back, despite ourselves, into profane time, still gasping from our glimpse of beatitude. We cannot do away with the everyday; sometimes we can divert or intensify it. *Real life is not absent, it is intermittent*, a lightning bolt that stands out against the gray dullness of the everyday and for which we feel a lingering nostalgia. Or rather there is no single "real life," but many possible interesting lives, and that is the good news.

It was the nobility of surrealism to glorify "the wonder of the everyday"[5] and to urge us to carry out a revolution

---

[5] "Will I long retain a sense of the wonder of the everyday? I see it being lost in everyone who moves through his own life as down an ever-smoother road, who moves in the habits of the world with increasing ease; who

in our way of seeing our environment. Poetry is not hidden in the heavens or in a hypothetical future, it is accessible to everyone, right now. Through, for example, automatic writing, which consists of dislocations and breaks that allow us to hear previously unheard sonorities in language but also glorifies everything we take for stereotypical: ordinary objects, posters, shop signs—over which our eyes and minds skate mechanically. We apprehend the world blindly, we can no longer discern its buried riches. Beneath the ordinary, we have to disentangle a breathtaking beauty. It is never the real but rather my view of it that is boring and that I have to disinfect, cleanse of its impurities.

Doesn't modern art involve a "transfiguration of the commonplace"?[6] On the one hand, it desacralizes classical artwork—painting, sculpture—by using the humblest objects and materials; on the other hand, it sublimates these trivial objects by ripping them out of their context, disorienting them, elevating any consumer product to artistic dignity, like Duchamp's urinal.[7] Sabotage on the one hand, promotion on the other: part of contemporary aesthetics consists in this reversal. The decline of the noble and

---

gradually rids himself of a taste for and the perception of the unusual. That is what I can have no hope of ever knowing." Louis Aragon, *Le Paysan de Paris* (Paris, Librairie générale française, 1966).

[6] Arthur Danto, *The Transfiguration of the Commonplace: A Philosophy of Art* (Cambridge: Harvard University Press, 1981).

[7] The irony is that other artists have been able to turn the provocation around and, like Pierre Pinoncelli at a 1993 exhibition in Nimes, urinate in the famous fountain in the form of an inverted urinal created by Duchamp in 1917 and strike the object with a hammer. Pinoncelli, who was the initiator of street "happenings" in France and was prosecuted for his activities, explained that through a converse procedure, he wanted to transform a work of art into an ordinary object, considering this an artistic performance.

pompous, the rise of the ugly and rejected. It is for the artist to show us that so-called common life is anything but common, to awaken us to its magical qualities. An aesthetic revolution is first of all a revelation that rejuvenates the world, opens up new perspectives on it. The ordinary is always the invisible exceptional, just as the exception is the ordinary exhumed. In other words, everyday life can be transfigured if each of us, at his own level, becomes a miracle-worker, a creator of Eden, a "divine killer of habits" (Pierre-Albert Birot).

The Prisons of the Calendar

Why do we go to school? First of all to learn to remain quiet and to be punctual, Kant said. The proper use of days and hours, that is what is first driven into our little blonde or brunette heads. Internalized since childhood, this acclimatization to regularity remains with us forever. We were turbulent and unpredictable, we become stable and assiduous.

This schedule is also reassuring because it makes it possible to control time, to give the days a framework and prevent them from scattering. It offers us the very special pleasure of converting a void into a fullness. If we cannot occupy the hours—no easy task—we can at least organize them down to the minute. "The construction of a schedule for this winter has taken me nearly eight hours in a row," wrote the indecisive Amiel. A perverse project of foreseeing life in order not to live it. The anticipation entirely exhausts the act: the attraction of imagining the future, enjoying its image without achieving it. We imprison weeks in the straitjacket of a program to be sure that at least we have a place in it, that we are expected.

Within calendrical restraints, as our new table of the laws, pathologies are now flourishing. Some people are always ahead or behind time: two ways of evading the rule, through an excessive punctuality that is almost insolent, and through a casual tardiness that is almost boorish (especially in a situation in which every minute is as long as a century: the lovers' rendezvous). There are people who pretend to be relaxed but are constantly looking at their watches and always seem to have some urgent task to accomplish. Not to mention retired people who rise at dawn and then wander about aimlessly, unable to free themselves from the reflexes acquired during their working life; or certain idlers who claim to be overworked and can't grant you a quarter of an hour without frantically flipping through their appointment books.

In the elaboration of a precise schedule we should not see solely an obsessive formality. At the heart of the most rigid subdivision of our days lies the hope of a dramatic surprise: as if we were protecting ourselves from the aleatory and at the same time dreaming that it might explode time's excessively tight links. Like guerillas who improvise airstrips in the middle of a field by painting white lines on the ground, we cut up our days and nights with rigor, hoping for an absolute surprise. This compulsive ceremonial nurtures two contradictory feelings: a pathological hatred of the spontaneous and the desire for a beneficial apocalypse that would abruptly sweep away our depression. We can think about a calendar the way we think about the mechanism of a watch: they are the bars of the prison, but they are also a promise of escape.

Gardening or Radicality?

Nonetheless, life can never be reduced to the alternation or inversion of altitude and platitude; between the two lies a whole range of small delights that it would be a mistake to scorn. More important than happiness, there is above all the joy of living on earth, embarked upon an ephemeral and mad adventure.[8] We can laugh about minuscule pleasures and find them too plebeian, too minimalist. Nonetheless, they include a large amount of truth and sanction the long history of the nobodies, the anonymous. They have the particularity of conflicting with two fixed ideas: that the common people are victims or rebels, never happy, and that their pleasures are ridiculous because they are gregarious, never original or unusual. This happiness of ordinary people—fishing, camping, do-it-yourself projects, household arts, gardening (and we know how the taste for gardens gripped Europe at the time when belief in the earthly paradise was waning)—can be dismissed, mocked; whole lifetimes can be spent showing that it doesn't exist, that it is a kind of illusion.

For a whole school of political thought, popular happiness is always the happiness of a slave who loves his chains, it is the complacent ignominy of the swine, wallowing in

---

[8] It is hard to accept a definition of joy as the unconditional approval of life, an absolute acquiescence in everything that is, *amor fati* (Nietzsche). Assent is close to resignation, and these propositions look very much like the sermons of the most retrograde zealots. Conversely, there is joie de vivre only if we discriminate between the odious and the delicious and refuse to accept things as they are. The power of saying "yes" has value only if we have the equivalent power to say "no."

his mire, both stupid and blissful. Since the people are crude, their ambitions have to be shown to be petty, their amusements risible, their dreams cheap. Subtle strategies of distinction and symbolic domination are for the powerful. Laborious imitation, endlessly renewed misery is the lot of the humble. Here there is no question of using education to raise the common people to the dignity of political actors. Instead, they have to be told how to live, their tastes have to be decreed to be pathetic, their mores backward, their fears ridiculous. And the critique of the redneck, the hick, or white trash by a certain part of the hip left-wing would be more credible if the critics recognized that they are themselves part of the group they discredit.

It is not the people in its diversity that is loved, it is radicality, that is, a mythology that is applied to the lower classes whether this pleases them or not. When the people betrays this vocation and appears in a form other than the two canonical figures of the fighter or the groaner, when it dares to claim small joys, then it is cursed, reduced to the level of a traitor to its historical mission. "The people do not know that they are unhappy, we are going to teach that to them," Lassalle said. "You are slaves who think you're free," cries the scandalized revolutionary to those who take pleasure in their humble fancies. Rather as Rosa Luxemburg was astonished every morning when proletarians did not take up arms to overthrow capitalist society, the troupe of do-gooders would like to make people ashamed of their little pleasures and of living their tiny lives instead of acting as the protagonists of a great historical narrative. There will always be intellectuals and politicians who want to treat our supermarkets, working-class suburbs, and ordinary ugliness as the gravest of crimes. That is exactly what revisionism (especially far left revisionism) does when it banalizes Nazism in order to Nazify capitalist and liberal banality.

Divine Unreason

Thus there is no salvation outside banality, or rather banality paradoxically constitutes both a hindrance to salvation and its condition of possibility (at the same time that it eliminates any hope of a definitive salvation). To dream about abolishing banality is to nourish, by pretending to be vehement, a fantasy of using stimulants to discipline the meager flock of days so as to extract the maximum number of sensations from it. Must we then declare null and void the life of elderly persons whose range of pleasures has contracted, but who nonetheless continue, despite their diminution, to experience many satisfactions? One cannot tear oneself away from the prose of the everyday by the force of will alone or by exhortation, and "the most delicious state has many listless intervals," as the *Encyclopédie* put it in the eighteenth century. The surrealists set out to reenchant the world, while the situationists tried to elevate ordinary life to great heights. But the slogan "Live without pauses and enjoy without constraints" has become the slogan for merchandise and information that circulate twenty-four hours a day, with neither pauses nor boundaries, just as the surrealist transmutation of the banal often degenerates into fakirism when it limits itself to gilding the pill and practicing a systematic embellishment. A bit of shine in the eyes and a great deal of grandiloquence do not suffice to make palaces suddenly rise up from the ruins of hovels. (It remains to be discovered why these two insurrections on the part of life—and the first, after all, had more brilliance and flair—very quickly declined into settling of scores, invective, and excommunication, as if the old human plague was taking vengeance on those who claimed to have done away with it.)

Despite what crusaders for incandescence say, there is no revolution against boredom: there are escapes and strategies for diversion, but the gray despot puts up a stubborn resistance. Boredom has its virtues: it prostrates us, but it also forces us to undertake things and allows us to develop more fully the unsuspected resources of time. In its torpor, it is sometimes a prelude to radical change. Without boredom, without that somnolence of time in which things lose their savor, who would ever open a book or leave his native village? There is everything to fear from a society of continual amusement that never fails to satisfy our slightest desires.

Robert Misrahi says, "A happy life implies a qualitative experience that combines satisfaction with significance, that is, an intense self-presence with a coherent meaning that is actually desired and realized."[9] It seems to me, conversely, that a moment of happiness is a moment taken

---

[9] Robert Misrahi, *Le Bonheur* (Paris: Hatier, 1997), p. 22.

away from the tyranny of meaning, a moment of respite in time, a temporary evaporation of concern. Being joyous, laughing or hugging people we love, doesn't *mean* anything, but it does us good. Why does happiness have to have meaning the way a lame person needs a crutch? With divine mischievousness, happiness provides us with satisfaction for no reason at all, bursting out like a fanfare or surreptitiously slipping between the days and then disappearing without warning. The greatest felicity is perhaps the one that is highly arbitrary, that is neither expected nor calculated, and that falls on us like a gift from heaven, suspends the flow of time, and leaves us disconcerted, ravished, stunned. (And we can also visit the humble home of our past and find there many moments when we were happy without knowing it.)

If happiness were really everyone's dearest wish, as we are constantly told, if we could decree it or catch it in a net, how can we explain the fact that just when they are about to attain it so many people manage to destroy it, to trample it as if they sense that such a victory would be worse than failure? As if they suspected that nothing resembles hell more than paradise, that the latter can be glimpsed but not achieved (drug addicts know that a rush of absolute pleasure quickly turns into the terrible thirst of need). If by some miracle all of our desires were to be realized in a single night, there would be nothing left for us but to waste away: that is why religion's promise of immortality is above all a promise of an eternity of numbed exhaustion.

The Two States of Festivity

Traditionally, religious holidays were moments of ex-hilaration in which a society inverted its hierarchies and plunged into chaos in order to tighten its bonds and re-generate time. Our individualist age has difficulty toler-ating these programmed joys and thinks it doesn't need official dates to show its play instinct. In the name of im-provisation, we all seek to amuse ourselves on our own, to awaken sources of fever beneath the surface of our too well-behaved lives. But to enliven ourselves we have to do more than reject obligatory periods of relaxation.

Take nightclubs, for example: these "houses of illu-sions" (as whorehouses used to be called) constitute a bubble of effervescence in the prosaic sequence of time and open onto an upside-down world that has its own codes, rites, and fauna. But they are also hysterical places where laughter and gaiety are always a little forced and that often provide a mechanical festiveness by means of noise, congestion, and smoke. The party animal is a kind of professional of the imponderable, a strategist of exuberance.

However, it would be a mistake to contrast this ava-lanche of artifices with an authentic, informal festivity. Over every gathering of people drinking, dancing, and feasting hangs the threat of failure, of half-heartedness, as if the gods had slipped away. The success of such gath-erings depends on a mysterious alchemy: in every joyful assembly there is an irresistible contagion that draws its raison d'être from itself alone. But when the party doesn't gel, when conversation flags, when all the necessary in-gredients—music, alcohol, drugs, sex—fail to produce the magical precipitate, then the temporary grace of festivity flips over into melancholy.

Besides the fact that the festive ideology is the counterpart of the doctrine of work (we are obliged to amuse ourselves the way we are obliged to work, to the point that in France we import other countries' holidays, such as Halloween), the mystique of the spontaneous no longer guarantees enchantment any more than does the strictest organization. An eternal paradox: as soon as it becomes its own pretext and refuses to feel emotions on command, festivity comes less easily. The spark doesn't want to ignite, and a taste of ashes spoils the finest parties. The revenge taken by the boring on night owls. We are not masters of our amusements; we need rules to arouse them, and we begin to mime jubilation in order to feel it. There is a whole strategy of spontaneity that resembles the rather rigid ceremonial of the carnivals and celebrations of yesteryear. Fervor cannot be commanded, and it sometimes disappoints us by not showing up for the appointments we have made with it.

To live solely for happiness would thus be to live for a few instants and throw the rest away. This also implies that unhappiness begins as soon as happiness stops, whereas most of life eludes this alternative, taking place in an inadequate middle ground consisting of minor annoyances, worries, little pleasures, periods of waiting, projects. Thus we are doomed to curse banality even as we accept it: it is the abyss that leads us astray and the grayness that guides the light. It hints at a miracle that it both displays and dissimulates. It is undecidable.

PART III

The Bourgeoisie,
or The Abjection of Well-Being

CHAPTER SEVEN

"The Fat, Prosperous Elevation
of the Average, the Mediocre"

I call bourgeois everyone who thinks basely.

—FLAUBERT

We are not fighting so that the people will be happy.
We are fighting to impose a destiny on the people.

—ERNST VON SALOMON

One Must Be Either a Monk or a Soldier

In 1995 two boys threw incendiary bombs into a fashionable restaurant in Colmar. The owner died in the resulting
fire. Arrested a few years later, the two young men, who
came from good families, explained that they had wanted
to strike a blow against a symbol of bourgeois order.

The bourgeois! Big or little, for two centuries he has
been the most hated and most reviled figure, a sort of abstract prototype of ignominy that has left its actual instan-
tiation behind and taken its position in the pantheon of

The quote in the chapter title is from Hermann Hesse.

accursed gods. The whole history of antibourgeois mythology is one long series of anathemas, from the Old Regime
merchant aping the aristocracy, clowning and dancing
in a grotesque manner, to the capitalist of the nineteenth
and twentieth centuries who profits from the sweat and
labor of the people. Violently rejected by the nobility because of his prosaic nature, by the working class for his
cupidity, by the artist who despises his way of life enslaved
to calculation and utility, the bourgeois is, so to speak,
characterized by an ontological baseness. Stingy, exploit-
ative, crude; the only quality lacking from this catalog of
negative traits was that of criminality, and since Hannah
Arendt we know that terribly normal individuals ran the
Nazi extermination machine.[1] The good husband and father whom Péguy declared to be the last great adventurer
of the twentieth century is now a potential monster inclined to commit the worst atrocities in order to gain a
pension and health benefits.

Since the Romantics and Nietzsche, the bourgeoisie has
had to answer to all camps for at least three offenses: *mediocrity, vulgarity, and rapacity, the three constellations of the
bourgeois cosmos*. One must be either a monk or a soldier,
Joseph de Maistre exclaimed, summing up in a formula the
whole grandeur of an Old Regime driven by a few fundamental passions. It was when the warrior and the saint declined that the bourgeois was born, entirely devoted to the
genteel commerce to which the Enlightenment assigned

---

[1] George Steiner adopted Arendt's hypothesis and developed it further in
his fine book *In Bluebeard's Castle: Some Notes towards the Redefinition of
Culture* (New Haven: Yale University Press, 1971).

the double task of exorcising violence and draining its energies through methodical action. It is self-interest, the French and English philosophers said, that constitutes the most social and most serene of pleasures: it pacifies mores and regularizes life. It focuses desire on a single object, the attraction of profit, and substitutes for unreasonable behaviors the prudence of accounting, the taste for acquisition, and the instinct for property. Combining virtues and inclinations, merchants became the true model for modern times: "Commerce cures people of destructive prejudices, and it is almost a general rule that wherever there are genteel customs, there is commerce, and wherever there is commerce, there are genteel customs," Montesquieu wrote, reproaching hermits and conquerors whose choice of extremes led them to be severe.

But before Marxists and socialists detected in this happy medium a shameless exploitation of the proletariat, the Romantics saw its pacification as a terrible narrowing of the human. Bourgeois morality had reduced desire to the stingy dimensions of material enrichment alone. Life might be calmer, but God, how small it was, especially for those who had experienced the splendors of the monarchy and hurricanes of the Napoleonic adventure. "Anyone who has not lived under the Old Regime does not know how sweet life can be." Talleyrand's famous aphorism confirms that many people experienced the entrance into the nineteenth century as a fall from grace, another exit from Eden. The earthly paradise promised by the Enlightenment had become a *terribly mundane paradise*. The new class of entrepreneurs and merchants promised a dull sort of happiness: outside the shop and money, there was no salvation. No more extremes, no more highpoints: humanity was supposed to devote itself to these two activities with the febrile monotony of a flock of sheep. Opposed to all excess, the petit bourgeois—a man who is, so to speak, small twice over—is the insipid being par excellence; even his tragedies lack glory and smell like the stewpot.

The crime of this new class? To have re-created destiny, whereas the revolution promised freedom, equality, and mobility. Collectively, by restoring, through social inequalities, a society of orders; individually, by forging a new human type that was docile and modest, identical in all situations. In a way different from the aristocracy, the bourgeoisie, despite its progressive values, revealed itself to be devoted to the notion that individuals and groups have fixed destinies. It gave rise to an unprecedented anthropological model, the standardized, mass-produced individual, a new collective subject fated to perform the same tasks, share the same desires, think the same way. To designate these undifferentiated multitudes, which he saw proliferating in the Russia of his time, Gogol invented the marvelous term *menuaille*, beings that can be called "ashy" because "their garments, faces, hair, and eyes have a sort of ashy surface, like a day when there is in the sky neither cloud nor sun."[2] This mass production of the same makes the human race a tamed species in which every individual is a copy of the others, a domesticated animal

[2] Nikolai Gogol, *Taras Bulba and Other Stories* (West Valley City, UT: Waking Lion Press, 2006), p. 336.

that has abandoned all impulses and passions in exchange for security and a dwarfish happiness.

What is fascinating about the works of Flaubert, Zola, and Chekhov is that they present individuals who seem to be free but who are dominated by the great constraints of fate, heredity, family, blood, money, and respectability. In an age of progress and optimism, these writers were birds of bad omen: poor or rich, alcoholic or healthy, their characters carry within them the fracture that will finally shatter them. Even the most recalcitrant, the free-thinkers, are sooner or later caught by the common law and mercilessly punished for having tried to escape order.[3] It was the genius of Chekhov, for example, to show us, with a soupçon of cruelty, ardent, rebellious souls, often those of women whose dream of glory and beauty is shattered by the hazards of life. Consider his plays and short stories: what counts is not what happens but what does not happen: "people don't love each other, don't get married, don't leave."[4] The three sisters imprisoned in their little town will never go to Moscow and experience a larger destiny, the fiancée who cries "I want to live . . . I'm still young and you've made me an old woman," full of spirit, says farewell to her family, certain that she is going to leave her native town forever—"as she thought," the author adds, hinting that this is a false departure. The Chekhovian hero is someone who rises to move toward freedom but always

[3] See Jean Borie, preface to Émile Zola's *La Curée* (Paris: Henri Mitterand, 1960), and Gilles Deleuze, "Zola et la fêlure," in his *Logique du sens* (Paris: Minuit, 1975).

[4] Wladimir Troubetzkoi, preface to Chekhov's *La Fiancée* (Paris: Garnier-Flammarion), p. 11.

stumbles and falls. Rebels are doomed to be ground up like other people. That is probably what Sartre meant when he made the bourgeoisie the equivalent of the passivity and even the viscosity of being, or when Paul Nizan described this class as "the world of failed lives" wholly "prey to death."[5]

War: Why Not? It Would Be Amusing!

The nineteenth and twentieth centuries responded to this general flattening out of ideals and behaviors with the dream of a shattering catastrophe, a revolution or war that would interrupt the excessively monotonous course of time. "Rather barbarity than boredom," Théophile Gautier cried in 1850, and his exclamation was to illuminate a whole period of rancor and disgust. Since life under the gray skies of the bourgeois order secretes the most fetid lethargy, the predatory morality of the aristocrat or the freedom of the savage proud of his body and his desires are preferable to it. War, a general conflagration, came to seem to many people to have all the attractions of the new and sensational, especially after the long period of peace Europe had experienced before 1914. Wearied by the uniformity and tranquility of their lives, European nations cherished the idea of an amusing apocalypse before they actually made it a reality.

[5] Nizan, *Antoine Bloyé* (Paris: Grasset, 1933).

As one young thinker put it in 1913: "War: Why not? It would be amusing!"[6] For many people, war not only was amusing but represented the most beautiful of syntheses, the combination of barbarian energy with feudal courage. In 1915 the sociologist Werner Sombart contrasted the shop-keeping mentality of the British with the heroism of the Germans, who were the descendants of the brave Teutonic Knights. In 1914 Adolf Hitler got down on his knees and thanked God that war had broken out because he saw it as man's natural fatherland, the supreme test that transformed the trenches into a "monastery with walls of fire."

In my turbulent youth, nothing afflicted me more than having been born precisely in a time that clearly erected its temples of glory solely to shopkeepers and government officials. The fluctuations of historical events seemed already to have calmed, and the future appeared to belong only to peaceful competition among peoples, that is, to a mutual, fraudulent exploitation that was accepted and excluded any method of self-defense by force. . . . [Thus when the war broke out in 1914] these hours were like a deliverance from the painful impressions of my youth. Nor am I ashamed to say today that carried away by a tumultuous enthusiasm, I fell on my knees and thanked Heaven with all my heart for having given me the good fortune to live in such a period.[7]

[6] Quoted by Julien Benda, *La Trahison des clercs* (Paris: Grasset, 1975), p. 211.
[7] Adolf Hitler, *Mein Kampf* (Nouvelles éditions latines), pp. 158–159.

To the vulgarity of the Nietzschean "last man" entirely devoted to his little pleasures, the whole twentieth century, from T. E. Lawrence to the Red Brigades via the Futurists and the Freikorps, has opposed the Romanticism of volcanic spirits impatient to lose themselves in "storms of steel" (Ernst Jünger) and trample on "that filthy culture."[8] We have to choose between being "hard or soft," as the theoreticians of National Socialism put it, we have to choose between the consistency of a block of stone or the inconsistency of gruel, we have to cultivate the "camaraderie of the machine," which will give us souls and hearts of iron.[9] Finally, we know how twentieth-century intellectuals, all of bourgeois origin, were fascinated by violence and brutality, and their taste for "limit situations" (Jaspers), their tendency, disguised as a concern for justice, to seek to bring about change by making things worse. "I want to live only in extreme situations. . . . Everything that is mediocre exasperates me so much I could scream," exclaimed Drieu La Rochelle excitedly in 1935, when he was on his way to Moscow after visiting Nuremberg and Dachau. Nine years later, in 1944, he noted in his journal how much he admired Stalin, the new master of the world who was stronger than Hitler.

The crime of the bourgeoisie? It prefers security to courage, mediocre survival to glorious death in a redemptive bloodbath. Bourgeois happiness is doubly detestable: for

[8] Quoted in Hannah Arendt, *The Origins of Totalitarianism* (New York: Harcourt, Brace, 1951).

[9] Alfred Hugenberg in 1928, and Kurt Schuder in 1940, respectively. Quoted in Peter Sloterdijk, *Critique of Cynical Reason,* trans. Michael Eldred (Minneapolis: University of Minnesota Press, 1987).

believers, it glorifies a materialism that pays little attention to spiritual salvation; for revolutionaries, it crowns the triumph of little, pusillanimous people who do not dare to put their lives at risk in the ordeal of the supreme sacrifice. Yes, better to be a terrorist or a criminal than a little bureaucrat or petty stockholder! And better Mao or Pol Pot, Castro or Milosevic, than the nauseating domination of the bourgeoisie. For some people, even Auschwitz is preferable to the cybernetic nightmare of our societies.[10]

We do not have to choose, thank God, between hell and platitude. War, as we know, is no longer in favor in the West; our armies have adopted—at least so far as they themselves are concerned—a "zero casualty" policy, and the twentieth century has perhaps temporarily immunized us against mass bloodbaths (but not against violence, which is rising more than ever). What has tarnished war's reputation is its very special combination of horror and boredom. Here it is fear that is thinking: waging war in order to keep monotony in check, it takes monotony to an unparalleled new level. And our contemporaries, considering their own lives more important than any cause, rightly refuse both routine and butchery and are immune to the poetic attractions of the abyss. But the biggest change in the West since the 1960s is the liberation of mores. That is what leads us to seek in sexual pleasures or in certain drugs the intensity that people earlier

---

[10] "And what lyricism there is also in the massacres at Auschwitz, when they are compared with the icy hands of generalized conditioning that reach toward the future society and are so closed to the technocratic organization of the cyberneticians." Raoul Vaneigem, *Traité de savoir-vivre*, p. 21.

sought in warlike enterprises, at the risk—but this another problem—of seeing pleasure annexed in turn to the realm of repetition (the great modern adventure is the inward one, the exploration of inner space). In other words, we have acquired *the right to live differently*, to escape the straitjacket of the single model. Shaken by challenges, the bourgeoisie has had to reexamine itself and accept the fact that it is not the last word on the human, the canonical shape of civilization. The artistic revolutions of the 1920s, the emancipation after World War II, and the rise of jazz and rock'n'roll marked the loosening of the bourgeoisie's terrible grip on society.

The same mentality of suspicion that had allowed the bourgeoisie to destroy the aristocratic sublime was turned against it, forcing it to open up, to see itself as it was seen by others. The bourgeois, who used to be "steeped in decorum," now no longer owes any allegiance to the collectivity and is conscientious by day and a party animal by night (Daniel Bell), combining neoliberal ethics with a frantic quest for pleasure inherited from the 1960s.[11] But above all, he has become the embodiment of the guilty conscience, rejecting in detail and in general the milieu from which he comes (for example, the whole work of the French sociologist Pierre Bourdieu testifies to the petit bourgeois's self-hatred, which leads him on the one hand to trample underfoot his class of origin, and on the other to practice, with regard to the upper spheres, the "masters

[11] As Mark Lilla has brilliantly observed in "La double révolution libérale: Sixties et Reagonomics," *Esprit*, October 1998.

of the world," a reverential disapproval, a hostility full of respect).

What is the mark of a bourgeois? He constantly bad-mouths the bourgeoisie, its odious respectability, its atrocious hypocrisy. So that self-denigration has become the bourgeois mode of being: because he belongs to a class that constantly has to relegitimate its existence and never cease to decry the principles it declares, he is forced to live divided against himself and to "recognize that his adversaries are partly right" (François Furet). That is why we are so shocked when European and American conservatives, echoing the crusading emphases of their predecessors, claim once again to regiment our mores and our private life, and to impose a single way of life on everyone. In this respect, what a contradiction to see in civil unions or in gay marriage with adopted children the forerunners of the disintegration of the family! It is exactly the reverse: it is the familial order that is triumphing over all of us, no matter what group or belief we subscribe to, and it is hard to see any argument, anthropological or other, that we could make against it. Moreover, let us note that although it is still endemic in the bourgeoisie, what used to be called bourgeois stupidity, the complacent pleasure of a clear conscience, and a strong adherence to oneself, has spread to its enemies, and affects any group, social category, and ethnic or sexual minority that takes pride in being what it is and displays itself with naïve satisfaction. People state their identities only to make others yield, and display them noisily, perhaps out of fear that without them they would not exist. It is as if for many of these movements, identity is a right to preferential treatment that excuses their faults and frees them from the discomforts of being forced to re-examine themselves, from the obligation to take a certain distance on themselves. Conformism and anticonformism amount to the same thing, and the discipline among marginal groups is in no way inferior to that in normal groups, especially when it adopts the alibi of rebellion.[12] Today, the bourgeois says he is an artist and assumes the pose of a subversive, of the great resister (opposing capital, the moral order, racism, fascism, censorship, etc.). Here antibourgeois vituperation is characterized by its attachment to the continued existence of the object it execrates. It vituperates not to kill but to preserve.

Bitter Triumph

By a clever or accursed irony, depending on your point of view, the bourgeoisie has not only survived its predicted destruction but proliferated to the point of becoming the new universal class, halfway between the very rich and the very poor, whereas the proletariat, the former messianic subject of History, is declining in numbers everywhere and being replaced by salaried workers whose jobs are not secure. In short, the bourgeois no longer has an Other,

[12] According to Lucien Sfez, in 1995, 45 percent of literature majors at Stanford said they were gay, a figure that has little to do with reality. The author sees three reasons for this phenomenon: it is cool to say you're gay and not to have the brutal image of the heterosexual; gays being a minority are protected by labor unions; and finally, gays cannot be accused of sexual harassment. *La Santé parfaite*, p. 65.

and his fiercest detractors, such as the artist, are only more or less picturesque variants of the bourgeois himself. Since the bourgeoisie has absorbed the ways of life that challenged it, class differences still exist, but within a single whole, and develop within a single sphere, but they are not for all that less ferocious. And this dominant mass itself is opposed to all the excluded groups that form on its boundaries a turbulent, rebellious aggregate and that are all the more bitter for not being, at the moment, the bearers of any project. If nothing escapes the immense octopus of the middle classes, we can still despise them, that is, we can despise ourselves, ceaselessly flagellate ourselves. Antibourgeois grievances are no longer political; over time, they have become cultural and even metaphysical.

The fact that we are all bourgeois in one way or another is shown by our religion of the economy raised to the rank of supreme spiritual good. It plays the role of an absolute, and it is in accord with its criteria that our contentment and uneasiness are now measured. In short, the economy, instead of being our tool, is now our destiny. From this derives *the modern conflation of comfort, well-being, and happiness* and our veneration of money: for we have all become Protestants in Max Weber's sense, we all believe in money's virtues and in money as a virtue (more exactly, this is a Puritan variant of Protestantism that grew up in America and has now spread to the entire world). It is perhaps the weakness of utilitarian doctrines that they postulate a sovereign good that everyone should seek and that they think it possible to harmonize people of goodwill. They have the merit of promoting a progressive politics that defends the achievements of the welfare state, but they lapse into constraint when they define its contents in a discretionary way at the cost of excluding anyone who does not abide by the rule: when, for example, it penalizes inveterate smokers on the ground that a man who destroys his health cannot be happy, or when it gravely discusses the fifty-five-mile-an-hour speed limit's repercussions on our personal happiness.[13] There is nothing despicable about these subjects; on the contrary, it took a real political and moral upheaval to give the common people access to creature comforts and conveniences. Let us recall that in the nineteenth century reactionaries thought it indispensable for social peace that the people remain afraid and deprived. But if governments can create optimal conditions and promote all sorts of ends that are good in themselves (health, housing, education, security), they do not have the right to decide what a happy life should be. People agree only about the evils to be avoided; they cannot agree on the supreme good, which is left, at least in a democracy, for individuals to determine as they see fit. We can discuss it ad infinitum, we can note with astonishment that many paths lead to delight, we can court others' agreement on the subject, but we cannot impose or decree. In other words, *there are politics of well-being, but there are no politics of happiness.* If poverty makes us unhappy, prosperity in no way guarantees euphoria and delight. That is the danger involved in making the pursuit of happiness a right: either it is diluted into a myriad of

[13] Charles Murray, *Pursuit of Happiness and Good Government* (New York: Simon and Schuster, 1988), p. 186.

subjective rights that ignore the common interest, or it is left to an oligarchy or the state to determine what is preferable, at the risk of lapsing into authoritarianism.

Villiers de L'Isle-Adam conceived an apparatus for collecting people's last sighs in order to make the death of our loved ones less cruel. Reich constructed a machine to accumulate "orgonotic energy." No doubt some group of scientists is currently building a "hedonometer" to gauge the GNH (Gross National Happiness[14]), the degree of beatitude in a given population, the way we measure the degree of humidity in the air. No matter how ingenious the calculation, we can count on the figures having little to do with "happiness," which lies outside the domain of statistics and need.

It remains that since 1989 the hatred of capitalism, far from decreasing, has been growing more intense, since in the absence of alternatives this system weighs on the world like an inescapable fate. It is not credited with any benefits, and it is considered responsible for all misfortunes. All the more because, while it has triumphed over communism, it has failed to keep the promises its theoreticians promised, since whole regions of the planet are left in deprivation and poverty. The only way to kill it would be to adopt it wholly and unanimously, so that it would perish under the burden of its contradictions. But it thrives on criticisms and gains renewed energy from them, assuring its permanent resurrection. It is an organism that is constantly mutating and regenerating itself in unexpected forms. In

---

[14] The term adopted by the Club of Rome in opposition to the GNP.

a strange twist, those who criticize it seek only to beat it at its own game or to outdo it. They think they are its adversaries, but they are merely its brokers; they think they are working to move beyond it, but in fact they are perfecting it. Whence the incantatory aspect of anticapitalist (or antiliberal) discourse, which consists of both anathema and aid, because by emphasizing the system's failings it helps the system reconstitute itself and avoid collapse.

Antibourgeois execration has a bright future: by means of this rhetorical figure, it is modernity as a whole that screams its self-hatred, repudiates its failures and its ugliness, and condenses the aversion it feels for itself. Modernity does not like itself (even when it disguises itself as postmodernity). It raised human hopes so high that it can only disappoint us. A bitter revenge for religions: they may be in bad shape, but what succeeded them isn't doing so well, either. I don't know whether we should fear, as some people say, the appearance of a transnational "hyperclass" (Jacques Attali) that would control the flow of wealth and knowledge and would establish a kind of apartheid on a worldwide scale. On the other hand, and in view of recent history, perhaps we should fear those segments of the bourgeoisie that, out of frustration and horror at themselves, are ready to ally themselves with the populace, as they did in the twentieth century, and to return to totalitarianism—naturally, in the name of social justice, the damned of the Earth, race, civilization, or some other camouflage. Let us beware of these elites that are bored, curse the pettiness of their lives, and covetously long for apocalypse and chaos.

The Dreariness of Promises Fulfilled

Lost illusions: since the Romantic period, they have been frequently contrasted with the heroic dreams of youth. Life is supposed to follow an inevitable itinerary from hope to disenchantment, a perpetual entropy. However, it is possible to oppose to this commonplace of dashed hopes another model: that of the blessed surprise, illusions rediscovered. The world of dreams, contrary to what is usually said, is poor and mean, whereas reality, as soon as we begin to explore it, virtually suffocates us with its abundance and diversity. "I call spiritual intoxication," said Ruysbroek, a Flemish mystic of the Renaissance, "the state in which pleasure transcends the possibilities desire had envisaged." To the principle of anteriority, which judges life in relation to a program, we must oppose the principle of exteriority: the world infinitely surpasses my ideas and expectations, and we have to get beyond them to begin loving it. It is not the world that is disappointing, it is the chimeras that shackle our minds. Answered prayers are dreary: there is something very profound in the wisdom that warns us never to find what we are seeking. "Preserve me from what I want," keep me from living in the Golden Age, the garden of wishes fulfilled.

There is nothing sadder than a future that resembles what we had imagined. We are disappointed when our wishes coincide with what we are experiencing, whereas it is especially moving to see our expectations diverted by particular incidents. (The literature of happiness is usually a disabused literature: hopes have either been betrayed or, more disturbingly, fulfilled, and desire satisfied, that is, killed.) Pleasure arises more from a project repeatedly thwarted and turned in a different direction than from a realized desire. While boredom is always associated with equilibrium, joyous overflow occurs when the imagination has to yield to the greater marvels of the real: "I had to choose between the hammer and the bell; what I remember now is mainly the sound they made" (Victor Segalen). Every inspiring life is both an achievement and a defeat, that is, a marvelous disappointment when what happens is not what one desired, and one becomes sensitive to everything that makes life opulent, fervent, and captious. The defeat of an illusion always opens the door to miracles.

In other words, it may be that we oscillate between two fundamental attitudes: that of the prosecutor who condemns life because he evaluates it in comparison with a utopia or preconceived idea (paradise, "a future that sings," happiness) and that of the defense lawyer who goes all out to celebrate both its disappointments and its attractions, whether it wounds us cruelly or caresses us softly. And when the accuser exclaims, "I've been cheated," the defender replies, "I've been satisfied."

CHAPTER EIGHT

What Is Happiness for Some
Is Kitsch for Others

A Bottomless Abyss

In the attack on democratic culture that has been going on ever since the French Revolution, there is one word that pops up over and over: *vulgarity*. This word, which is of recent origin, appeared at just the time when the people ceased to be subjugated and became, nominally at least, the main actor in political life. It spread with the social mobility that led to a confusion of the classes, putting on an equal footing the noble and the commoner, the city-dweller and the peasant, the proletarian and the boss, and producing the terrible dissonance that arises from mixing different social milieus and separate castes that have not been able to maintain their positions. Vulgarity seized the world as soon as aristocratic virtues and the people's child-ish innocence both disappeared, to the advantage of that unpredictable object, the middle classes, which took up a position equally distant from the extremes and claimed to guarantee moderation and institutions, in accord with a schema developed by Aristotle, the philosopher of the human middle.[1] But they are also a site of mobility, a zone of impure alloys in which earlier divisions are blurred. Everything that is middle is not necessarily mediocre: it is also mediation, a place of confluence and the convergence of exchange. And the middle classes can be defined in terms of leveling, equilibrium, and permeability.

It is no news that the common people are naturally crude. Before becoming synonymous with martyrdom or insurrection in the socialist Christology, the people initially designated a primitive state of consciousness. In the *Republic*, Plato compared the people to a "large animal" that has to be carefully petted to tame it, an ignorant, stupid animal whose role in the conduct of a state is comparable to that of a ship captain who is deaf and myopic in matters of navigation. Under the Old Regime, two kinds of humanity lived side by side without contaminating each other; impermeable barriers separated the common people from the rest of society. With the disappearance of the feudal world, everything changed. But although the people has in principle gained sovereignty, its taste is still considered suspect. Thus Kant explained that the Savoy peasant, who is too rustic, cannot grasp the beauty of the glaciers and peaks, in which he sees only danger

---

[1] "In every state without exception, there are three groups of citizens: the very rich, the very poor, and those who occupy the middle ground. If we grant that only the moderate and happy medium are worthwhile, it is clear that it is best to enjoy worldly goods moderately as well. That is how one can most easily obey the dictates of reason" (quoted by Jacqueline de Romilly, *Problèmes de la démocratie grecque* (Paris: Hermann, 1975), pp. 177–178. The middle class, according to an argument later adopted by Michelet and Raymond Aron, is neither rich enough to lapse into idleness nor poor enough to revolt.

and distress. The commoner, the serf, the villein, whose souls, it was believed in the Middle Ages, left their bodies through the anus, and whose deaths made people laugh in medieval epics, have perhaps become the main figures in the affairs of the city but remain by nature incapable of perceiving the sublime. If they tried to meddle in such matters by giving their opinions, they would sink into stupidity.

Vulgarity is not the awkwardness of the uncultivated boor, the classical object of aristocratic mockery; it begins with Molière's Bourgeois Gentleman, who mimics the noble he will never be, and this marks a crucial turning point: the invasion of the masses into manners and mores, in other words, the elevation of the inferior to the same rank as the superior. It is a result of equality, a symptom of a time that claimed to destroy hierarchies, to replace the well-born by the meritorious, to give everyone the same chance. Values are flattened out, distinctions erased; the society lady can turn out to be a whore, the most elevated dignitary a low adventurer. Vulgarity, to adopt an expression Zola used in referring to the Second Empire, is an orgy, a mixture of genres; it is a rush toward easy pleasures, the amalgamation of orders and prerogatives, universal association, the crush of appetites and ambitions; finally, it is the triumph of the parvenu (and of his corollary, the pariah), of the illiterate millionaire who hastens to acquire the rudiments of polite behavior and culture in order to throw a modest veil over his origins.[2]

[2] Émile Zola, *La Curée*, summarized by Jean Borie in his preface to the novel, pp. 21–22.

A Happiness Gene?

In the 1970s a team of researchers in neuropharmacology, investigating the effects of cocaine and opiates, tried to identify substances whose varying presence in the brain determined whether an individual had the gift of good humor and a sense of pleasure.* Referring to a "hedonic capital," they described depression, frigidity, and tension as specific neurological states. Investigation in these domains has continued down to the present day. No one will deny that we have differing, genetically determined aptitudes for pleasure, stress, pain, and aging. But are these decisive factors? If there were really a happiness gene like the—completely fictitious—genes for crime, fanaticism, or homosexuality, what a relief that would be! Life would cease to be a chaotic history that we write in accord with circumstances and acquires all the rectitude of a program: no longer inscribed, as it used to be, in the great book of God, but in the branching of our DNA. We would be calibrated for a certain degree of satisfaction, marked by our chromosomal baggage, no matter what we did or wanted. There would be, on the one hand, anxious people forever condemned to adrenalin and serotonin, and, on the other hand, the blessed whose brains are perpetually flooded with dopamine. We would no longer have worries due to freedom and chance: we would be genetically predisposed, thus predestined.

But the great mystery of happiness is that it cannot be reduced to components that allow it to emerge or prevent it from emerging: even if they are optimally bundled together, happiness transcends them all, does not allow itself

---

* Edward Khantzian, Paul Meehl, and Donald Klein, quoted in Giulia Sissa, *Le Plaisir et le mal* (Paris: Odile Jacob, 1997), pp. 168, 169.

to be isolated or defined, and disintegrates, like a butter-
fly's wing, as soon as we think we have grasped it. Above
all, however, life always has the structure of a promise, not
that of a program. To be born is in a sense to be promised
to a promise, to a future that shimmers before us and that
we do not know. So long as we see the future as unpredictable and unknown, this promise has a price. It is the peculiarity of freedom to take existence somewhere other than
was expected, to foil biological and sociological codes.
The excitement of not knowing what will happen tomorrow, uncertainty about what awaits us, is in itself superior
to the regularity of a pleasure inscribed in our cells. In any
case, it is a value that far transcends happiness, it is the
romantic, that marvelous power of destiny to keep surprising us right up to the end, to astonish us, to knock us
off the rails we were running on. To a happiness that lacks
history, shouldn't we prefer a history that lacks happiness
but is full of new developments? There is nothing worse
than those people who are perpetually cheery no matter
what the circumstances, who have pasted a radiant smile
on their faces as if they were sentenced to a life of joy.

The Usurpers' Strategies

Vulgarity is a perversion of imitation, a malady of legiti-
mation: it always consists in pretending to be something
one isn't. Instead of pursuing a patient process of learning,
the vulgar person puts himself in the place of the person
he is imitating and claims to equal if not dethrone him.
Thus vulgarity follows the history of the bourgeoisie like

its shadow and casts doubt on its finest conquests: this class not only has betrayed its mission by re-creating a Third Estate beneath it but has also bowed down before those whom it defeated by borrowing ways of life and fashions from them. The nobility fascinates the bourgeois because it possesses a grand style that they will never have; they copy its manners with an assiduity that borders on the grotesque because they hope thereby to provide for their existence a foundation in tradition that it lacks.[3] The imitator thinks he has caught the essence, but he has remained on the level of appearances and bogs down in parody. He cobbles together signs he does not understand and seeks to affiliate himself with the caste he desires by aping it. Excess instead of simplicity, noisy ostentation instead of distinction, that is what betrays the commoner who wants to assimilate himself to the aristocracy.

That is why vulgarity is intimately connected with money, that is, with the temptation to purchase elegance, class, and the respect that one does not have by birth, and in this respect the nouveau riche is emblematic. In his attempt to convert the grammar of possession into the language of being, he goes too far, betraying his origins at the very moment that he is trying to make people forget them. No matter what he says or does, he lacks the nonchalance, the presence of mind, and the easy manner of the well-born. With his too-well-tailored clothes, his falsely relaxed comments, he always looks like he's trying to impress people And his pathetic efforts cast him back

---

[3] See Philippe Perrot's excellent study, *Le Luxe* (Paris: Seuil, 1995), esp. pp. 163–167.

into the shadows from which he so much wants to emerge. What the parvenu learns at his own expense is that he is not distinguished because he is rich, and he is not one of the rich because he has money: he is an individual who has succeeded, that is all, and who is dying to be recognized by those in high places. *There are people who have money, and there are people who are money;* the heirs of a noble lineage, and the needy who will always lack education, the patina of time, and refinement.

How can we fail to see, however, that the nouveau riche's crudeness is a sign of vitality, a factor of movement?[4] What disturbs people about the parvenu is less his insolence than his insidious corruption of codes: he profanes the models he venerates. To be copied is to be dispossessed, to have one's legitimacy challenged, almost to be overthrown. In this respect, for many people the absolute capital of vulgarity is America, that delinquent child of Europe that has outdone its parent. In the nineteenth century Schopenhauer already wrote that

> The specific characteristic of the North American is
> vulgarity in all its moral, intellectual, aesthetic, and
> social forms: and not only in private life, but also
> in public life; it sticks to the Yankee no matter what
> he does. . . . It is this vulgarity that opposes him so

---

[4] Although in France there is no lack of sociological studies of new money (Michel Pinçon and Monique Pinçon-Charlot have provided a very good overview in *Nouveaux patrons, nouvelles dynasties* [Paris: Calmann-Lèvy, 1999], to my knowledge nothing has been written on the enormous success of the French who returned from North Africa, on their fusion with the old bourgeoisie, and on the ostentatious luxury they sometimes show off and that attracts some people as much as it horrifies others.

absolutely to the Englishman: the latter always seeks
to be noble in all things; and that is why the Yankees
seem so ridiculous and repulsive to him. We could
rightly say that they are the plebeians of the whole
world.

It remains to be discovered why these plebeians have
contaminated the rest of the world with their way of life
and why the American saga has imbued the whole planet
to the point of becoming in its turn an object of universal imitation. We have to acknowledge that in vulgarity,
that is, in the awkwardness of aping, there is a formidable
energy, a work, whose result is often the creation of something new. *It is one of the paths that novelty takes in order to emerge.* The strength of American vulgarity is that,
combined with a spirit of building, it has broken all ties
with models and that, in its excessive imitations of other
cultures, it has invented something never seen before, a
new civilization.

For Saving Kitsch

According to a rumor that has been circulating for at least
a century and a half, modernity, which has succeeded
politically, is an aesthetic failure that has resulted in the
domination of the small over the great, the petty over the
noble, the slovenly over the harmonious. Stuffed with useless objects, modern man is supposed to have traded the
graces of the mind for the gewgaws of amusement. Since

no class or elite now determines canons and norms, the mercantile and media subculture is left free to impose everywhere its approximations, simplifications, and foolishness. This view is not entirely false. Vulgarity is in fact the symptom of a society that is inhabited by nothing but itself and claims to accord legitimacy to all collective or individual expressions. It is the counterpart of popular sovereignty from the moment that the latter, exceeding its jurisdiction, claims to exercise its authority in manners and the arts. That is why, if we do not want to transform democracy into a spiritual defeat, we have to protect the sovereign people from itself, from its infatuations, from the mass culture it imposes by the sheer fact of its numerical dominance. We have to colonize, to the benefit of democracy, values traditionally considered restraints on its expansion: fervor, revolt, grandeur, intransigence. To endure, democracy needs its own antithesis, which might kill it but can also revive it. Therefore it must be inoculated, in homeopathic doses, with the aristocratic or barbarous virtues that conflict with its ideals, we have to declare "the war of taste" (Philippe Sollers), reestablish gradations, confound the silly and the mediocre, and demand everywhere the restoration of a hierarchy of style and talent.

Similarly, we have to reinvent codes of polite manners in a culture of immediate contact: for example, we need to reject the habit, borrowed from America, of addressing strangers by their first names and if possible by their nicknames. In this regard, the paradox is that America, opposing the formalism of manners inherited from the

Old World, has re-created in turn a *formalism of spontaneity*, of immediate, excessive cordiality that seems to a foreigner the height of hypocrisy (especially when the "niceness" subsequently turns into indifference). Politeness is a small politics, an artifice accepted to avoid aggressiveness, ease human intermingling, and recognize the other's place without infringing on his freedom. It is urgent to rediscover a civility that is able to reconcile deference with flexibility, to re-create simple rules and to include in them, why not, the old gallantry, tact, and the "principle of delicacy." There are modes of common life other than stuffy stiffness, pseudo-connivance, and boorishness.

Nonetheless, there is a dizzying aspect to vulgarity, an abyss that calls to us and repels us at the same time. Contrary to mediocrity, which levels, and sentimentality, which euphemizes, there is in vulgarity a will to wound, to shock, to give voice to the powers of the underworld, the dirty and the ignoble. There is, of course, an erotic use of vulgarity that turns to the benefit of the flesh the malediction pronounced on it, takes pleasure in humiliating the high by the low, allows fantasy free rein, and takes a delicious joy in this humiliation. And we know how disturbing we find the coexistence in some people of a good education and wild behavior, of a superficial angelism and an actual nastiness, even timidity allowing the emergence of an underlying bestiality. In the same way, there is a whole aesthetics of kitsch that goes from Clovis Trouille to Jeff Koons (La Cicciolina's ex-husband) by way of Pedro Almodóvar and the French television show *Les Deschiens*, a whole stupid, mean culture that uses and abuses bad taste to turn official inanity against itself (just as some slasher or pornographic films play with nudity, blood, and the body seen as a piece of meat in order to unhinge the spectator). Not to mention the Garden Gnome Liberation Front, whose goal is to take these little plaster dwarves, unjustly imprisoned by their owners, back to the forest where they belong. After all, Flaubert's Bouvard and Pécuchet thought the best way to fight bourgeois stupidity was to copy it down, line by line, out of revenge. Flaubert's head spins when he is confronted by stupidity, that modern form of the infinite: to demolish the happy imbecile, you have to become an imbecile yourself, but an unhappy one.

This excess of saving vulgarity, which is supposed to cleanse us of social dirt, is an explosive material that may contaminate its users in turn. Bad taste is a vocation that is not without its dangers; and just as lovers can always sink into a routine crudity, that is, into the ridiculous, there is a very fine borderline between subversive vulgarity and the complacent vulgarity it is supposed to challenge. (And similarly, taking the cliché to the second degree, as Andy Warhol and pop art did, is often another way of amplifying and thus exonerating it.)

Vulgarity is like idiocy: to get rid of it, you have first to recognize it in yourself, to acknowledge its vague seductiveness, and not project it onto others. It also marks our attraction to the imitation, the fake, the garish, all those counterfeits that pretend to be real and end up corrupting the real (just as the multitude of fake blondes makes us doubt there are true ones but leads us to look for the true fake blonde). The only tolerable vulgarity is one that is unaware of itself, disguises itself in the faded finery of elegance and bon ton, and condemns crudeness in others. Everyday life is always kitsch, always associated with a bric-a-brac of ludicrous dreams, with universal knick-knacks. *That is why some people's happiness is always other people's kitsch*; as soon as a way of life is adopted by the middle classes, it is immediately abandoned by the upper classes. Thus there is a good way of using vulgarity as a mental hygiene against the world's obscenity, a detergent to wash away idle chatter by reinvesting clichés to draw from them new sources of surprise, of strangeness; but it is also a trap that can be fatal. This "negative grandeur" of democracy is both a lucky break and a curse: it guarantees the mobility of forms and destinies, but it expands the empire of junk and the counterfeit to include everything. The battle against it is endless: it re-creates itself as it is attacked, infecting those who think they are proof against it, and the more it is underestimated, the more it reigns. Thus there is no possible redemption or escape in high culture, the fine arts, small, select societies, or the pure aestheticism in which elitist passions currently like to take refuge. Everything is always already compromised: we are doomed to undergo vulgarity, to fight it and love it, to play with it like a sword that protects us and kills us. We have to raise a barrier against shit, Flaubert said, thundering against the trinkets of the Second Empire. This is a program we can still undertake. On the condition that we admit that this "shit" attracts us and that we are in it up to our necks.

A Whole Life Well Failed*

"A successful life," Vigny said, "is an adolescent dream come true in adulthood." The Greeks saw it rather as a reflective life, dedicated to thinking, a life that flourishes by having larger goals and that can offer an example for everyone. For my part, I would say that a successful life is one whose richness is taken for granted, whose fulfillment is obvious, and which, no matter how modest it is, we would not exchange for any other because it is our own.

But if all destinies are not equally valuable, should we conclude that some are worth nothing at all and ban those that do not meet our criteria? The assessments are sinister, even the positive ones that require us to adopt the point of view of death: it is death that will settle accounts and make us prey to others' judgment. "A man cannot be called happy until the last instants of his life," said Solon. But so long as we are still breathing, it is unjust to subject us to the alternative of victory or defeat. Just as Christopher Columbus failed to find India but discovered America, we are constantly "failing" but accomplishing something else, a peculiar adventure that continues until the final moment.

It is because every life is a lost cause that it can be both good and noble in an indissoluble mixture of glory and decline. Not being necessary, it needs neither to succeed nor to fail, it limits itself to being pleasant. There is a certain grandeur, an unacknowledged generosity in certain worldly defeats, whereas admirable careers are accompanied by aridness and desolation. Our certitudes in this area are negative: I don't know what a good life is, but I

---

*Pierre Autin-Grenier, *Toute une vie bien ratée* (Paris: Gallimard, 1997).

know what a bad one is—it's the one I don't want at any price. Don't tell me what a successful life is, tell me about your own life, tell me how your failures were transfigured into something that makes sense for everyone. If we can't help asking the question, we mustn't answer it, for fear of limiting the range of possibilities and sterilizing them.

We all know people loaded with honors and medals who experience these decorations as a premature burial; they have been classified forever. Let us avoid conclusions, leave people the possibility of falling, getting up again, and going astray, without imprisoning them in a judgment. There is a certain truth in the theory of reincarnation: it is in this world that we can experience several lives, be reborn, begin over again, take a different path. What matters is to be able to say "I have lived," and not "I have vegetated." We are never saved or damned; and we will all die "somewhere in the unachieved" (Rainer Maria Rilke).

CHAPTER NINE

If Money Doesn't Make You Happy, Give It Back!

Are the Rich the Model of Happiness?

In a striking passage, Proust describes the dining room at the Grand Hotel in Balbec as an

> immense and wonderful aquarium against whose wall of glass the working population of Balbec, the fishermen and also the tradesmen's families, clustering invisibly in the outer darkness, pressed their faces to watch, gently floating upon the golden eddies within, the luxurious life of its occupants, a thing as extraordinary to the poor as the life of strange fishes or mollusks (an important social question, this: whether the wall of glass will always protect the wonderful creatures at their feasting, whether the obscure folk who watch them hungrily out of the night will not break in some day to gather them from their aquarium and devour them).[1]

We have all witnessed such scenes in European spa cities, where we see vacationers crowding around yachts

The quote that forms the chapter title is from Jules Renard.

[1] Marcel Proust, À l'ombre des jeunes filles en fleur (Paris: Gallimard/ Pléiade, 2000), 1:681. Translation by C. K. Scott-Moncrieff.

and greedily watching marvelously relaxed millionaires in shorts drinking cocktails. Wealth is first of all a spectacle that gladdens the eye, whets the appetite, and heightens resentment. As if the rich also needed to be recognized by those who have nothing and were to receive everything, even the appearance of general approval.

For a long time, the upper castes of our societies embodied the alliance of savoir-vivre, beauty, and good manners; they were not only without need, they raised the human race to a previously unimagined degree of refinement and extravagance. Alongside this image, another cliché was established: that of the unhappiness of the Great. Rich people are bored: forced to remain inactive, they are supposed to be tortured by emptiness, not knowing how to kill time, which they spend frantically searching for new pleasures. Their life-weariness is a way of atoning for scandalous fortunes, and they are both unhappy and guilty: unhappy with their idleness, guilty of living parasitically on people who work and suffer. The idleness that ought to be their pride— only commoners are doomed to be punished by having to work—becomes their curse. These "kings without amusement" are slowly dying of inanity amid their golden splendors. This was a convenient cliché: it allowed the deprived to endure their condition, since that of their masters was infinitely more difficult. It is pointless to envy them or to overthrow them: they are already in hell!

Our age has put an end to this dual fable. On the one hand, the rich are not unhappy—or if they are, it has nothing to do with their bank accounts—and they are certainly not repentant. Has anyone ever seen a millionaire on his knees begging forgiveness on the eight o'clock news? On the other hand, ignoring class barriers, the world of work has grown much more extensive, and working does not prevent people from being bored. In this respect, one of the perversions of unemployment may be to have restored to labor, even the most stultifying, an aura it had lost during the years of prosperity. Obsessed by full employment, our societies want to keep people busy at all costs, and they celebrate wage slavery without looking into the quality of this employment. To the point that working too much has become an outward sign of power, and whereas the working classes aspire to idleness, the so-called idle classes are increasingly busy, boasting that they work sixty to eighty hours a week, and brandishing overwork as a sign of their superiority.

When it was shared by very few people, money seemed to embody all the world's wonders. The extension of comfort and well-being to the majority of the population has replaced both poverty and great wealth. The possibility of getting rich or at least achieving a comfortable way of life, which is now open to everyone, has both accelerated envy and banalized a universe that used to seem so prodigious. The nabob is a poor man who has succeeded, especially when we see new technologies making so many young people millionaires by the age of thirty.[2] We continue to

[2] This is the phenomenon of the million-dollar babies. At the beginning of the 1990s, there were seven thousand millionaires in Great Britain; by the end of the decade there were twice as many (*Courrier international*, October 1999). According to an American author, at one point sixty-four people a day were becoming millionaires in Silicon Valley (David A. Kaplan, *Silicon Boys and Their Valley of Dreams* (New York: William Morrow, 1999). In France, according to *Le Nouvel Économiste*, thirty-three new multimillionaires appeared in 1999.

spy on the lives of the powerful; we now doubt that felicity resides exclusively with them. We can admire their tenacity, their entrepreneurial boldness, the brilliant idea that propelled them out of obscurity into the limelight, their ability to sense opportunities. But it is not from them that we draw the substance of our aspirations. Who, for example, dreams of being a French or American employer, the head of a firm whose life seems to be about as much fun as that of a pencil-pusher? Their lives, which are as regulated, well behaved, conjugal, and familial as one could want, are as boring as those of any employee: they are less great, free-spending lords than petits bourgeois with a lot of money.

There is another reason why the "feasting of these marvelous creatures" described by Proust no longer makes us salivate: people get rich in order to keep to their own kind, to enter an exclusive club where battles are fought with symbols and trophies. The first thing the wealthy do is to surround themselves with servants, interposing between themselves and the world a cloud of intermediaries. Here a dual principle of visibility and segregation is operating. Forced by their position to adhere to codes and a rigorous morality, they maintain a relationship of loyalty to traditions that has slackened elsewhere. If we except a few eccentrics, accession to the apex of the pyramid usually results in discipline and conformism: high society is doomed to be a ghetto.[3] Not to mention the fear

[3] According to Michel Pinçon and Monique Pinçon-Charlot's pertinent analysis of the traditional bourgeoisie on the west side of Paris, *Dans les beaux quartiers* (Paris: Seuil, 1989).

of being loved only because of one's bank account and becoming prey to gold-diggers. That is why the nabobs' residences, no matter how flamboyant, become gilded hells when they have to live, as they do in Latin America, barricaded in their fortresses for fear of attacks or kidnappings. Their homes will always lack the permeability, the openness, that characterize places where there is creation and pleasure. What the rich feel compelled to do—isolate themselves in their residential neighborhoods, keep their distance from ordinary people, and close their doors to the unexpected—seems to us the height of tedium. *The world of capital is dreary* because it is not the world of exchange but that of closure and autism. As if money, like an insatiable divinity, circulated day and night only the better to freeze and petrify those who have it.

If there are desirable milieus today, they may have to be sought on the margins, in the contagious minorities that used to be excluded and that by their culture and music now set the tone for the majority. The middle classes seek elsewhere, sometimes on the fringes of legality, thrills that they no longer find in their own mirrors. The strength of the marginal is its exoticism, which makes it both dangerous and attractive: by violating the rules, it escapes the ambient uniformity. In general, the more a society invents lifestyles that escape the attraction of the wealthiest classes, the more dynamic it is. And during the great periods of emancipation of the twentieth century in France, there were moments when official happiness, that is, the current conformism, was depreciated in favor of other ways of living together.

Fitzgerald, or Salvation through the Rich

Jazz, gin, Hollywood, the Côte d'Azur, surprise parties, wit, youth; and also alcoholism, madness, poverty, failure, becoming a bum, psychological problems. F. Scott Fitzgerald's work oscillates between these extremes in accord with a tendency that fascinates us by its inexorable aspect. From the outset, his drama is based on a belief that is as crazy as it is implacable: the rich are God's elect and form within humanity a luminous caste that no one can frequent without danger. In Fitzgerald's work, decline is contemporaneous with the dream of glory: happiness is a treasure concealed behind a heavy door that everyone wants to open. But no one succeeds in doing so unless he is well-born; and the fall is all the more radical because the intruders thought they were infiltrating the citadel. Even love, especially love, constitutes the illusion par excellence of those who want to transgress the rigorous order of the classes. That is why female beauty is an ambiguous promise. The ravishing heiress, the one who will, if you seduce her, help you move from the realm of darkness to paradise, is also the first to dismiss the suitor from a humble background and send him back to his origins. The beautiful woman with a voice full of money, the one about whom Fitzgerald writes: "Her manners revealed with great assurance that the beautiful things of this world belonged to her by virtue of a natural and inalienable right." She is the paradigm of a universe that tolerates no misalliances, a universe in which all the Gatsbys of the world are sent away once they have amused the audience. The conclusion is final: "Poor boys mustn't think of marrying rich girls"; when one takes "people out of their milieu, it turns their heads, no matter what they claim."

Because for Fitzgerald money is a divine talisman and social barriers are metaphysical barriers, the poor man, guilty simply because he is poor, has to be punished for his temerity, for having even dared to rise to another level. His inevitable defeat is devastating, a precipitous fall accompanied by the wealthy's mocking laughter. Fitzgerald's tragedy, his "flaw," resides entirely in the stubborn, puerile belief that money is a sign of election, and his novels are characterized by a Calvinism that divides the predestined from the losers. Poverty is a punishment, and the poor's brief moments of happiness are a usurpation because the rich have exclusive property rights to joy and pleasure. That is why in Fitzgerald the romantic problem is connected not with a passional or sentimental logic but with a socioeconomic one. And the dismissed lover, entirely occupied by his disgrace and faced with millionaires and their mountains of diamonds, has no choice but to drown his shame in alcohol.

Fitzgerald's whole work is a magnificent allegory of the American Way of Life and its frenetic worship of the almighty dollar during the 1920s and the Great Depression. But his modern epigones, fascinated as he was by the power of the wealthy, show us that this mentality is still very much alive. If the middle classes were destroyed in America, as some fear, leaving the well-off and the disinherited facing each other, then the America and perhaps the Europe of the twenty-first century might resemble the world of Fitzgerald's novels: a world imbued with the glacial theology of the dollar, the divine seal that distinguishes the elect from the damned.

The Preferable and the Despicable

Without entering into a debate that would be out of place here, let us say that money is one of society's "necessary immoralities," on the condition that its reign be restrained and controlled. It does away with all hierarchies connected with birth and social status except one, which cannot be transcended: the hierarchy of money. Let us first be wary of anyone who trumpets his scorn for the golden calf: we can be sure that in his heart he cherishes it or dreams only of taking it away from others. Money, and this is its advantage, remains a way of preserving individual freedom, of "cleansing social relationships of any affective adherence" (Philippe Simonnot), of achieving a certain autonomy. It has allowed, and still does, persecuted people to survive in dispersion, in exile, and is the portable homeland of those who have no homeland. Finally, as Spengler put it, "a highly evolved civilization is inseparable from luxury and wealth," and it was the magnificent role of patrons, from the Medicis to the Rothschilds, the Camondos, and the Pereires, to transmute base metal into works of art, that is, into a form of beauty and generosity. There is nothing uglier or more twisted than some Christian doctrinaires' praise of poverty as if it were by itself endowed with a superior virtue. Involuntary poverty that combines privations and humiliations, adding shame to need, is detestable. In all circumstances, money is to be classed among the "preferable things" (Seneca) that it is legitimate to have if fate has put you in a position to have them.

Pace its detractors, money's indecency does not lie in its existence but in its rarity, in its insolent confiscation by a handful of people; money is what almost everyone lacks, and the main problem is that it is unequally distributed. (A disagreeable feeling warns us that poverty in developed countries may never be overcome, simply because the rich no longer the need the poor to get rich. The relationship of subordination that made the worker's labor the condition for the owner's wealth has been replaced by a relationship of innovation and prospecting on the lucrative territories of "the new economy." The misfortune of being exploited has been succeeded by the still worse misfortune of no longer being exploitable.) Thus we have to go back to the ancients and acknowledge with Aristotle that wealth, beauty, and health are also accessories useful for a good life, even if they are not identical with it. "No one has condemned wisdom to be poor," Seneca said. "Although I have nothing but scorn for the empire of wealth, if I have the choice, I will take the best it can offer me." Even if base metal is the universal whore that transforms everything into merchandise, including the human person, even if we have to constantly remember the existence of values and feelings that cannot be bought, "the utopia of a world without money is one of those ideals the world really needs but which it would be dangerous to make the foundation and principle of the social order" (Leszek Kolakowski). Need we add that the greatest massacres of the late twentieth century, in Algeria, Rwanda, Timor, Bosnia, Kosovo, and Chechnya, were connected less with financial or economic issues than with religious, racial, ethnic, or imperial fanaticism?

A Virtuality without Limits

That said, we have to acknowledge a fundamental uneasiness: it is impossible to scorn money, and it is impossible to venerate it. Both money and happiness are abstractions and potentially represent the totality of possible enjoyments. With money, I can possess things virtually without being encumbered by their materiality. Moreover, there is a happiness in making money that is often superior to the happiness of having it at one's disposal: the happiness of taking a shortcut: making a nice pile very rapidly. If making a living is a drag, getting rich quick is a game that approaches erotic frenzy. But the problem is that money presents itself as a way of life in itself, a substitute for all beatitudes. When it is raised to the rank of an idol, an absolute goal, it becomes so desirable that it makes everything else undesirable. The elimination of obstacles is its strength and its tragedy: it pulverizes them, makes everything immediately accessible, but this omnipotence leads to indifference. By trying to grasp too much we grasp only wind and end up in a paradoxical frustration that prevents us from enjoying anything at all.

We know the comic character of the rich man who no longer has time to spend all the money he piles up, who has so much wealth that he is sated by the world and experiences a shortage of pleasure amid abundance. He would almost like to be able to start over from zero, begin the exciting climb up the social ladder again. Such people have, as we say, everything they need to be happy but are not. Since they have everything, they no longer have anything; their desire dissipates instead of focusing, it is always attracted by another mirage and always disappointed. Since they can no longer succeed, all that remains is for them to fail, to sink into the abyss, like those great dynasties so favored that they attract misfortunes and cataclysms. Money provides a marvelous illustration of the following paradox: *everything done to achieve happiness can also drive it away.* That is why a mad attraction to lucre has become, in America at least, a collective passion. "The most laborious of ages, our own, doesn't know what to make of its labor and its money except more money and more labor" (Nietzsche).

In our societies a very fine, imperceptible line separates money as an end from money as a means, and consumerism and advertising constantly seek to blur this line. Then at least the most robust of us enter the sphere of the "conspicuous consumption" that Thorstein Veblen saw in the mores of the upper bourgeoisie, that of the Rockefellers and the Vanderbilts, before World War I. Mansions, yachts, expensive cars, vast apartments: we are doomed to compete with others of the same rank to dazzle or at least equal them, that is, to envy anyone who has more success, and to disdain those who are struggling to catch up with our standard of living. When a CEO pockets a salary a thousand times higher than that of his employees, he is not displaying his competence or his merits, but a pure will to power refracted through his "remuneration." His pleasure consists in walking off with something other people don't have and impressing his peers. The problem with these rivalries is that you always find somebody richer, there's always some magnate whose splendor offends you, who comes in ahead of you in the *Forbes* or *Fortune* rankings, and whose wealth puts yours to shame. Here we have to distinguish the rich from the superrich and the ultrarich; these are different categories. Whence the terrible aridness of the wealthy when they don't put their riches in the service of some cause, some idea or art; they leave the impression of having failed to achieve any of life's goals.

A New Morality of Frugality?

In the end, there are a few moments in life when money regains its fluidity as a pure medium, when we have enough cash to allow us to dispense with calculation and not worry about tomorrow. *Money goes along with joy in life when we forget it, when it disappears as such,* and we can both possess it in moderate amounts and let our minds wander where they will. Not to be dependent on money is to know that you wouldn't live otherwise even if you had a lot more of it. But most of the time, everybody calculates, even the wealthy (the avarice of the rich, the fear of need amid the superfluous, is an astonishing symptom: for example, J. Paul Getty, a California oil millionaire who put a pay phone for guests in his London mansion and never left a meeting first so that he wouldn't have to pay the taxi fare). Most of the time, for most people, money is

comparable to drugs: it is supposed to free us from worries, and it becomes an obsessive worry, an end in itself. It
worries us when we don't have it, and it burdens us when
we do; it prevents us from having a proper relation to it.
The appetite it arouses is so stubborn that it makes pleasure
difficult if not impossible. That is what William Burroughs
says he learned from morphine: an insatiable desire puts
pleasure out of reach. Money becomes a sad passion when
it supplants all others and turns to rumination. And the
madness it elicits is seen in certain forms of speculation
and is connected with the romanticism of large numbers:
in a universe in which everything is calculated down to
the penny, it becomes a pleasure to defy calculation by
the enormity of the sums put at risk. There comes a time
when frantic calculation becomes gratuitous, absolutely
useless. The thirst for profit has been left behind, and we
are dancing on the edge of the abyss, getting drunk on the
poetry of numbers, and the stock exchange itself is transformed into a temple of mathematical exuberance. Like
the Internet, money is a constantly expanding galaxy in
which new planets are always being found; it is a carbon
copy of the cosmos.

In other words, if no one can claim to be comfortable with money, that is because *it is not reliable*, and it
works both for and against our pleasure. Hence it must be
rehabilitated—especially in a country like France, where
hypocrisy with regard to it and the hatred of vocational
success continue to reign—only the better to avoid the
traps it sets for us. In America, for example, in a context

of increasing inequalities and poverty,[4] new moralities of frugality are flourishing; in the name of a rational management of needs, they reject the institution of credit, loyalty to an employer, and the obsession with leaving an inheritance.[5] Is this a simple media effect, a temporary contrition before beginning new orgies of acquisition and consumption? Maybe. But it is symptomatic that at the heart of the financial system there arose a doubt as to its well-foundedness and a plea for a more ample life less enslaved to the logic of objects and to artificial covetousness. The real question is this: what price are we prepared to pay to have money, and what place do we want to give it? If we do not want to be possessed by our possessions, as the ancients put it, it is preferable to limit our expenses, if that allows us to satisfy our passions, to increase our share of real amorous and spiritual life instead of going deeper and deeper into debt.

[4] According to an American study, differences in income have constantly grown larger in the United States over the past twenty years. At the top of the scale, one American in ten has seen his income rise by 115 percent since 1997, and at the bottom one in ten has seen his income decrease over the same period. The middle classes are said to have seen their capital increase by only 8 percent (*International Herald Tribune*, September 6, 1999). The disappearance of the middle classes, which have gradually become proletarianized, would certainly signal the end of the democratic system for which they provide the foundation and the victory of an unbridled capitalism deprived of any counterweight.

[5] See Stephen Pollan and Mark Levine's provocative book, *Die Broke* (New York: Harper Business, 1997). Pollan, who is a financial analyst, sets forth the commandments for good management in the twenty-first century: tear up your credit cards and pay cash, mentally resign your job as soon as you start it, never retire, and above all die broke, distribute your property to your children while they are young and need it. And write a check to the funeral home for your burial. Coming from an investment guru, such a work signals the disenchantment of part of the American middle class with the policy of systematic downsizing in businesses and tries to put into practice a kind of internal abandonment of the system's postulates.

But above all, we must reestablish hierarchies and oppose to cash other sources of wealth that are cultural, aesthetic, and spiritual. Even the desire for glory and grandeur, even vanity, are sometimes preferable to the desire for gain, and to the mediocre constraints it presupposes. And the power of the great upheavals of the preceding century in France, including those of 1936 and 1945, consisted not only in redistributing the social pie, but also in creating new kinds of opulence for the majority of the people: free time, poetry, love, the liberation of desire, the sense of everyday transfiguration. Not being content to manage penury, but discovering everywhere new goods that are unquantifiable and escape the rule of profit, prolonging the old revolutionary dream of luxury for everyone, of beauty made available to the most humble. Today, luxury resides in everything that is becoming rare: communion with nature, silence, meditation, slowness rediscovered, the pleasure of living out of step with others, studious idleness, the enjoyment of the major works of the mind—these are all privileges that cannot be bought because they are literally priceless. Then we can oppose to an involuntary poverty a voluntary poverty (or rather a voluntary self-restriction) that is in no way a choice to be indigent but rather a redefinition of our personal priorities. This may involve giving up things, preferring freedom to comfort, to an arbitrary social status, but for a larger life, for a return to the essential instead of accumulating money and objects like a ludicrous barrier set up against fear and death. In the end, true luxury is the invention of one's own life, mastery over one's destiny; "but everything that is precious is as difficult as it is rare" (Spinoza).

The Fall of the Stars

Why do we examine with an unhealthy curiosity the love affairs, breakups, and tribulations of the people we call "stars"? It is because these exceptional beings, who need only appear to be, and whom we recognize even if we don't know them, these beings who can break any taboo and indulge in any excess, are venerated only in order to be subsequently reduced to the common level. Condensing in themselves the largest quantity of social desire, they should function to help us escape the empire of monotony; but they disturb the latter only the better to confirm it. And celebrity magazines may exist only to reassure readers, to confirm them in the idea that princes and movie stars are ambivalent embodiments of happiness, of an ideal that they are struggling to realize. Whence our bitter delight in seeing them having the same problems we do.

These "happy few" who are supposed to sublimate our destiny, take us away from our ridiculous worries and insignificant problems, show us that no caste or superior class experiences beatitude, which is the province of the gods alone, as Aristotle said, whereas "men are as happy as a mortal can be." And they show us that in the end a secretary can have the eventful and tumultuous life of a princess, and a princess can lead the conventional, homebody life of a housewife. That is what the democratic process is: the orgies and debauchery of the ancient monarchs are now accessible to anyone. Through the indiscretions of the media, we see with relief and sadness that these people are not essentially different from us: thus these same media also constitute *machines for controlling envy*, and beneath their apparent futility they perform an essential function. In her flashy pantheon, the starlet may escape anonymity, but she nonetheless succumbs, as we do, to confusion, solitude, and age (the gradual disappearance of beauty in lovely actresses is an obligatory rhetorical figure in a certain kind of periodical that notes it with a sadistic sorrow). We elect stars and politicians, and we forget them with the same indifference, the same fickleness. Our appetite for gossip and details does not have its source, as we have said, in alienation or dispossession. The cult of celebrity draws directly and contradictorily on the advance of democratic equalization.

PART IV

Unhappiness Outlawed?

CHAPTER TEN

The Crime of Suffering

Help me get rid of the pain that's making me suffer,
but let me keep it so I can exist.

—A PATIENT TO HIS THERAPIST,
   Revue française de pyschosomatique, no. 15

In a novel published in 1872, Samuel Butler imagines a
country, Erewhon (an anagram of "nowhere"), where
sickness is punished as a crime and the slightest cold can
land you in jail, whereas murder is considered an illness
that deserves to be treated with concern and care. With
acute foresight, Butler goes so far as to explain that grief
and distress—for example, the loss of a dear one—are
punished as a serious crime, the bereaved person being
no more than a delinquent guilty for his sorrow. A judge
sentences a man accused of pulmonary consumption to
life imprisonment at hard labor and explains, "If you tell
me that you had no hand in your parentage and education, and that it is therefore unjust to lay these things to
your charge, I answer that whether your being in a consumption is your fault or no, it is a fault in you, and it is
my duty to see that against such faults as this the commonwealth shall be protected. You may say that it is your

misfortune to be criminal; I answer that it is your crime to be unfortunate."[1]

This is a superb and ironic intuition that the second half of the twentieth century confirmed because it took, more than any other period, a gigantic step toward the negation of misfortune and the "prohibition of death" (Philippe Ariès). It is as if the whole period had sought to prove right the philosopher Alain, an indefatigable eulogist of the optimism of the Third Republic, who, in his *Propos sur le bonheur* (1921–1923), denies all reality to extreme suffering. For him as for Epicurus, it does not exist, it is impalpable, "horror is soporific," and when death strikes, it is instantaneous, leaving no place for imagination and fear. In this spiriting away, he goes so far as to maintain without irony that a man who is going to the guillotine "is no more to be pitied than I am"; all he has to do is think about something else, "count the bumps or turnings." As for Pascal, his shiver when faced by the stars and the infinite "probably resulted from having caught a chill at his window without having noticed it."

The Propagation of Trash

Since the Enlightenment, our societies have set themselves the task of establishing happiness on Earth, and we have been endlessly cataloging misfortunes to be eradicated.

---

[1] Samuel Butler, *Erewhon, or Over the Range* (London: Cape, 1921), p. 117.

But sufferings, like the heads of the mythical hydra, keep growing back. The more we track them down, the more numerous they become; the list gets longer every day, forcing us to postpone indefinitely the promised felicity. For a long time, the revolutionary movement liked to describe concerns connected with the fear of death and loneliness as futile and had only scorn for doctrines that dared to allude to them. All that mattered was that exploited workers overthrew current socioeconomic structures and seized power. Once capitalism, the source of all iniquities, had been overthrown, a new world in the service of humanity would emerge, and suffering would gradually recede like the tide. Things did not work out this way, as we know: not only did actual socialism multiply misfortunes everywhere it was imposed, but it left untouched all the problems inherent in the human condition, which it regarded as "petit bourgeois."

However, in dealing with the same subject, liberal democracies, though more prudent, have adopted a no less ambiguous attitude. If they prefer the long time of reform to the fast time of revolution, they continue to hope that a magical conjunction of science, technology, and material progress will succeed where totalitarianism failed. During the second half of the twentieth century, Europe was characterized by a feverish enthusiasm and inordinate optimism in which even mentioning misfortune was considered old-fashioned, not to say obscene. In our time, misfortune has been the object of the worst of conspiracies: a conspiracy of silence. Antiquity pinned its hopes on a refutation of suffering,[2] Christianity pinned its hopes on exaltation; we pin ours on denying suffering, we avoid it like the plague, and refuse to even consider the possibility that it might be real.

Grief, pain, and sickness thus remain unexamined in modern secular ideology and have acquired the unenviable status of residues in a society moving toward the future: events that are sidelined, forbidden to appear in speech or elsewhere, and with which everyone has to come to terms in his own way. But it is not suffering that has vanished but only its public expression (except, let us repeat, in literature). We have to simulate energy and good humor in the hope that if we conceal affliction it will finally disappear by itself. Confronted by it, *we don't know what to say*, especially when we think we have the perfect explanation (the logic of the market, sexual misery, poverty, etc.) that would cover the whole field of human suffering. We have banished it from our vocabulary just as we banish the unhappy, the wounded, and the dying who challenge our prejudices, "break the mood." Just seeing them undoes us because we have elevated youth, health, and fun to the rank of metaphysical idols. Since Tolstoy we have known

---

[2] Socrates: "For a good man, there is no misfortune either during his life or after his death." Epicurus: "Death does not exist for us." Epicurus again: "The wise man smiles when being tortured." Zeno: "There is no misfortune other than vice and shame." Epictetus: "There is no place for evil in the universal order." Epictetus again: "Do not ask that what happens happen as you wish it to. But wish that things happen as they happen and you will be happy." In his *Tusculan Disputations*, Cicero mocks these verbal quibbles and reaffirms the reality of pain. To construct for themselves an inviolable sanctuary beyond the reach of the world's tribulations: that was the ambition of some ancient philosophers and Eastern sages.

that suffering is dirty and death a nauseating annoyance; the nineteenth century rejected it in the name of decency,[3] and the twentieth repressed it in the name of pleasure. But whether it is in the name of good manners or the hedonist ideal, it remains the supreme impropriety.

There is a terrible blindness of happiness, which sees everywhere only its own reflections and wants to become the sole valid narrative. But just as in the consumerist universe trash ends up invading every space and reminds us of its existence in countless nauseating ways, suffering, unable to express itself, has begun to proliferate, increasing our awareness of our vulnerability. On the pretext of doing away with it, we have sacralized it. Having become a taboo, a gray zone in our societies, it has literally exploded, like a gas that has been too long confined; penetrating all the pores of society, colonizing territories where we did not expect to find it. The worst thing is not being able to say what's wrong with you, whether in the workplace or in everyday life, not seeing it accepted by others; this is a way of suffering twice over (just as, Philippe Ariès noted, the repression of tears and grief in mourning aggravates the trauma of loss). The West's error, in the second half of the twentieth century, was to give people the mad hope that an end would soon be put to all calamities: famines, poverty, disease, and old age were supposed to disappear within a decade or two and a humanity cleansed of its

---

[3] "The awful, terrible act of his dying was, he could see, reduced by those about him to the level of a casual, unpleasant, and almost indecorous incident (as if someone entered a drawing room diffusing an unpleasant odour)." Tolstoy, *The Death of Ivan Ilyich*, trans. Aylmer Maude, in *The Death of Ivan Ilyich and Other Stories* (New York: Signet Classics), pp. 134–135.

age-old ailments would appear at the gateway to the third millennium, proud of having eliminated the last traces of hell. Europe was supposed to become, as Susan Sontag profoundly put it, the sole place where tragedies would no longer occur. (And in every decade, every transition in the century, we heard the same drunkards' resolutions, the same old promises: borders are going to disappear, hunger will be ended, prisons abolished, diseases controlled, etc.)

Not only was this fairy tale not realized, but in a certain way it strengthened what it was supposed to eliminate. People had rightly denounced the culture of resignation propagated by churches and the bourgeoisie, especially in the nineteenth century. At that time, effort and endurance were considered normal, the price to be paid for sin or poverty, and pleasure was considered a rarity, a private garden surrounded by high walls and forbidden to the common people. But when hedonism is established as an absolute value, death and suffering become pure absurdities, intolerable assaults on our rights. They are not only ravaging but also useless, which makes them an even bitterer pill to swallow. And we get impatient with their persistence because we have been told that they would soon disappear. "Let us acknowledge the existence of evil without adding to the uglinesses of life the absurd smugness of denying that they exist," said Voltaire. Hence the paradox already mentioned: our societies have never talked so much about suffering as they have since they have been exclusively concerned with happiness. Through a fantastic reversal pain, which is supposed to have no legitimacy, has come to play an inordinately great role, in fact, the greatest.

Consider the dark luster currently enjoyed by the word "suffering." Confronted by it, everyone bows down: it is a passport that opens all hearts, suspends all judgment, excuses all crimes. It was François Mitterrand's genius to have staged his own death, several years before it occurred, in order to get away with the lies and omissions of his government. To confess, at the threshold of eternity and when one is courageously fighting a fatal disease, that one has sinned, is to make the confession anodyne, to disclose secrets in order to silence critics. It is no longer a leader who is speaking, it is an inhabitant of the beyond who is addressing us with the pallor of a cadaver, waving away youthful mistakes—working for the Vichy government, compromising friendships—by admitting them. If the classical death agony was exemplary, it was very indulgent and allowed the old socialist monarch, an expert in deception, to use his present suffering to gain a pardon for his past errors. A magnificent exit that conflicted with the morality and principles of democracy but provided a textbook example for playwrights.[4]

Because it was long relegated to oblivion and modestly omitted from political discourse, suffering is resurfacing, with a fanfare, and acquiring a dubious sacredness: far from being obscene, it is onstage, and when it is exhibited it is equivalent to absolution. The rules of ordinary ethics can no longer be applied to someone who claims to be suffering and displays all his stigmata in public. That is because

[4] On the death of heads of state and that of François Mitterrand, see the essays in comparative ethnography published by Jacques Julliard, *La Mort du roi* (Paris: Gallimard, 1999).

democracy is ambivalent about suffering: because it rejects it, it makes it the basis of rights that are always being newly discovered. Its great issues are first of all negative: reducing poverty, putting an end to inequality, fighting disease. An inevitable contradiction is involved in the designation of the problems we are trying to do away with. If all suffering gives someone a claim to a right and provides a foundation for the latter,[5] physical or psychological pain gradually becomes the measure of all things. To do away with pain, one has to first name it, make it exist. Since the Enlightenment, the range of what is considered unbearable has been expanding: what was previously seen as a matter of course is now seen as unjust, arbitrary. What has changed in comparison to earlier centuries is not the total number of our afflictions but our intellectual attitude toward them. *To be modern is to be incapable of playing the hand we are dealt.* The hatred of suffering is thus the source of every growth in rights, including animal rights.[6] And since the modest expectations typical of ancient times have given way to rising desires, we live in a state of constant aspiration that is constantly disappointed: no one is ever loved, gratified, or rewarded enough. For the Christian, the wages of sin was death; for us happiness should be the reward of existence, a kind of manna equitably distributed to all of us in gratitude for our being born. But the more immoderate the ambition, the more the result seems meager, and the range of the intolerable never ceases to grow. Democracy,

---

[5] Jean Poirier, ed., *La Douleur et le Droit* (Paris: PUF, 1997).

[6] As is shown by the controversial book by the Australian utilitarian, Peter Singer, *Practical Ethics* (Cambridge: Cambridge University Press, 1999).

generating a perpetual dissatisfaction, turns into a system for recognizing complaints. It is through the legal profession, which has become, as a jurist has said, "an immense labor union against suffering," that suffering has returned to public discourse: outlawing it paradoxically ensures its continual renascence. Here the hunter is the prisoner of his quarry, not the other way around.

Thus we have arrived at a worrisome confusion of adversity and unhappiness: the obstacle is no longer the usual resistance that the world opposes to our enterprises but a personal offense that deserves compensation. We confound the painful and the unpleasant, the unfortunate and the arduous; at the slightest opposition we cry: nobody loves me, everything is against me. The growing uncertainty regarding the places of suffering and nonsuffering causes new distresses to arise every day. Things that used to be accepted no longer are, and anything that impedes or delays satisfaction is considered a misfortune. A traditional category like physical effort—except in its ludic form in sports—is banned; and hard labor and unpleasant tasks are left to immigrants (an immigrant is someone who does not measure his effort). But intellectual effort has also been annexed to the domain of oppression: that is the problem with the schools that, seeking to respect chidrens' sacrosanct freedom and to spare them any vexation, often don't attempt to transmit anything: learning is assimilated to persecution, we have to help students blossom, not impose abstract knowledge on them.

In short, misfortune is no longer clearly delimited, it has invaded and conquered everything that is not pleasure in the strict sense, advancing by swallowing up conditions and emotions that were not previously associated with it. As a result, we have lost our sense of proportions; we raise the smallest displeasures to the rank of tragedy. We enter into an intoxication with pathos, which is no longer a strategy of distinction with respect to the bourgeois, as it was for the Romantics, but a reflex of systematic lament, a philosophy of day-to-day despair. The contemporary hell is not knowing where pain begins or ends; pain takes all forms and extends to the very fact of living, thus reviving a religious postulate we had thought obsolete.

Toward a New Culture of Suffering?

In an earlier book[7] I showed how the status of victim has become an enviable one, sometimes becoming hereditary and creating family lines of pariahs exempted from any duty and granted every right, and how the Hegelian war of consciousnesses has been replaced by the war of sufferings that clash on the public stage. How every people, minority, and individual fights to occupy the position of the maximal victim at a time when the traditional oppressed are seen as privileged, a confusion that leads to a rivalry in victimhood among Kurds, Jews, Bosnians, Tutsis, blacks, American Indians, women, gays and lesbians, and others who are competing for the honor of being the supreme martyr. How in our countries a market for suffering has

[7] *The Temptation of Innocence: Living in the Age of Entitlement* (New York: Algora, 2000).

developed that is connected with the extension of legal rights, a veritable demagogy of distress in which each person competes with others and flaunts his honors by displaying his sorrows. How this intoxication with misfortune, the result of a loss of confidence in human powers, has led to an unparalleled promotion of the jeremiad but also to the corruption of ordinary language, the nauseating juxtaposition of our little problems with great atrocities, the immoderate use of the word "genocide," and the systematic invocation of Auschwitz being the best indications of this bidding war.

Fortunately, not every problem is doomed to such a fate. Western societies may be groping their way, alongside the law as an instrument of reparation and political combat as well as a factor of justice, toward a relationship to suffering, and this may prove to be a fundamental revolution. The first stage consists in recognizing, after so many years of repression, that misfortune and suffering are constitutive of the human condition, in relearning to live with it in order to escape lethal traps, and to do the best we can with it. To make suffering part of our lives again, to reintroduce it into the common language, is to free ourselves from the unhealthy fascination it has for us when it is concealed, and to give ourselves the means to contain it by integrating it. We have no lack of competing recipes for coping with suffering. In addition to the two traditional recourses already discussed, those of the antiquity and Christianity, moderns have multiplied meaning-giving therapies, not to mention our massive pharmaceutical arsenal and all the bodies of wisdom, medical traditions, and exotic religious denominations that our confused age untidily calls to its bedside.

In this regard, a sophism is proposed by Buddhism and some Stoic schools that *offer to solve problems by dissolving them*. By decreeing that our attachments are fatal, our concerns vain, our selves illusory. By proposing peace of mind, serenity, by withdrawing from the tumults of society. If we think, conversely, that an authentic life resides not in renunciation but in passionate attachment to others and to the charms of the world, then these doctrines that assume that difficulties can be resolved by escaping them have little to teach us. If for us the worst of sorrows is to lose a loved one, only a person who has chosen the "ascetic ideal" (Nietzsche) will find much consolation in reacting to such a loss by saying, like Epictetus: "Never say about anything: I have lost it. Say instead: I have given it back. Your wife died; she has been given back. Your child has died; he has been given back." Between bland ataraxy and the storms of love, we may prefer the latter, even if by doing so we multiply the risks of being exposed to the blows of fate. Thus love, while it is the source of the greatest felicities, is in no way identical with happiness because it includes in its spectrum an infinitely broader range of feelings: ecstasy, dependency, sacrifice, terror, slavery, jealousy. Being the most thrilling and also the most dangerous of experiences, it can cast us into the abyss and raise us to the summits. Above all, it assumes that we agree to suffer for the Other and because of him, because of his indifference, his ingratitude, his cruelty.

There is both a confusion and a profusion of reference points: there is no longer any consensus—if we suppose that there ever was one—when faced with distress, for now we are used to selecting among different paths, one after the other, simplifying them if need be. A total relativism: it is up to each individual to deal with his own problems, in accord with his convictions and his means (and we know how much socioeconomic inequality aggravates the vulnerability to certain pathologies and increases discrimination in access to and the quality of care). It is no longer customary to endure ordeals as other people do: that may have been an imperfect response, but it had at least the merit of being collective and requiring a cathartic ritual. And just as Freud said that the goal of psychoanalysis was to teach us to put up with ordinary life, we have to get used to suffering again, "make it a neighbor," as Montaigne said about death, in order to rediscover a certain detachment with regard to it and attempt, so far as possible, to keep it at a distance.

Doctors and Patients

There is no figure more ambivalent than the doctor, who is simultaneously a preacher, a magician, and a healer, the master of both life and death. For a long time the image of him oscillated between two extremes: that of an arrogant practitioner intoxicated by his power and endowed with all the attributes of knowledge; and that of the family doctor, the tutelary divinity of French society who knew how to combine sound, precise diagnosis with friendly advice about what to do. Then the medical relationship was truly "the encounter between a conscience and a confidence" (Louis Portier), and these doctors, because of their loyalty, became almost guides capable of inspiring both physical and mental hygiene.

Everything changed when medicine became specialized and liberalized. In the hands of a specialist, not only is the human body fragmented, but each part of it is subject to competing authorities. The result of this new status is that in dealing with a physician we oscillate between faith and absolute suspicion. Since he is supposed to know everything, a doctor has no right to be mistaken. And some hypochondriacs wander nomadically from one doctor's office to another seeking advice or a new medication. The contemporary patient is a skeptic who does not believe in any treatment but tries them all, combining homeopathy, acupuncture, sophrology, and allopathy, a little like new converts who embrace several religions to increase their chances.

The more we expect from medicine in general (and today we ask everything of it, including the impossible, total recovery and victory over death), the more we grow impatient with the limits of doctors in particular. Medical science's individual servants are crushed under the weight of its promises, becoming commonplace and losing their authority; they are simple service providers who can be sued—often justifiably, moreover—if they commit an error. While the medical researcher, the scientist, and some surgeons whose skill amounts to genuine artistic genius retain immense prestige, in many cases the doctor is now seen only as a repairman who gets the machine running again until the next breakdown.

However, it is not clear that we are doomed to this fragmentary medicine, which often seems more like plumbing. Sometimes, fortunately, a communication is established between patients and physicians that is not merely utilitarian and allows the former to talk about their suffering, to make their symptoms part of a personal history. Then the relationship, instead of being inegalitarian, a relationship between a mandarin who orders and a patient who obeys, becomes an exchange and a contract in which two actors who are conscious of their limits try together, in mutual respect, to achieve the best cure possible. Perhaps the future lies in a union of the specialist's competence with the human understanding of the general practitioner.

Connecting by Sharing an Ordeal

The second stage of this revolution consists in bringing people together on the basis of their common tragedies. We no longer claim to eliminate misfortune at a single blow, as revolutionary socialism used to do, but to eliminate it bit by bit when it afflicts us. Every trauma, accident, terrorist attack, or epidemic gives rise to specific responses, to committees and associations in which a dual effort of mutual aid and exchange is made. People from all parts of society, from all backgrounds, happen to find themselves united by the same wound and, seeing the limits of medicine and psychiatry, decide to form a group to fight their battle together. It was the great innovation of Alcoholics Anonymous to have inaugurated a behaviorist theory based on the drinker's taking responsibility for his dependency, assisted by sponsors who have gone through the same ordeal and survived it. Thus is reactivated, against intemperance, an ideal of self-mastery under the supervision of monitors who protect and supervise. Drinking (or drugs) continues to be the center of life, but the relationship to it is gradually changed. Instead of drinking, members talk about drinking, and talk about it not to drink. What is lost in being weaned away from alcohol is regained in freedom, and people save themselves along with others through the very thing that was destroying them. Those who thought they had found a friend in alcohol and then saw that this friend turned against them have discovered in the group's rules a way of restoring their lost autonomy.

Something tiny but decisive may have changed in our relationship to illness. We fear it and avoid it as much as ever, but we are no longer willing to be dispossessed of it by an outside authority, whether medical or other; henceforth we demand to be associated as much as possible in the process of caring for ourselves. In this domain AIDS is no doubt a special case: since we could not cure it, for a long time we limited ourselves to denouncing those who suffered from it. The latter were initially mainly homosexuals and drug addicts and had to literally invent a social, legal, and political parade to resist ostracism and scorn, going so far as to re-create pagan funerals to bury their dead. A stupefying example of men and women subject to a common fate whose collective activity could have a beneficial effect on the way we deal with all other health problems. AIDS not only revived the old association between sex and death (even if at first it was haughtily underestimated and dismissed as a plot against the gay minority). It brought into confrontation two universes that no longer had anything to do with each other, youth and the tomb, at the end of a century that had promised us all that we would live, if not forever, at least to the age of 120. It came to taunt our maddest hopes, throwing us back into a kind of medieval horror because behind it generations of viruses were waiting in the shadows to kill us. But more than anything, it put an end to the myth of medical omnipotence and restored a terrible meaning to the word "incurable"—the most indecent word in modern language—and increased our panic with regard to the return of fatal diseases.

By that very fact, AIDS acquired a special status, half-political, half-medical; all pandemics are not, so to speak, so "beneficial." By the strong feelings it has aroused and the imprecations made against it, this one has forced us to make a new start. It has obliged researchers to pursue new directions, patients to change their status, and society to reconsider pathologies previously thought too shameful to discuss. It is perhaps thanks to AIDS, a sinister cymbal clap that shattered our complacency, that patients have become legal and social actors (and no longer simply passive objects in the hands of physicians) who can initiate lawsuits, as we saw in France in the affair of contaminated blood supplies, determine in accord with doctors what the best therapy is, and sometimes have a seat on the administrative boards of hospitals. Now responsible for the care he receives, the patient not only learns medicine at the same time he learns about his illness, but he also becomes an adult and participates in his own way in curing himself. In a Swiss clinic for children with cancer, every day the lethal cells are drawn on the blackboard and the children repeat: "I will kill you, cells, I won't let you kill me." By bringing his private drama into networks of friends, each person becomes both the manager of his illness and a teacher who educates others, teaching them to gain possession of medical and legal knowledge. This is a sovereign act of reappropriation, a passage from subjection to rediscovered dignity.

Thus it is sharing suffering and wanting to free ourselves from it that create the link and lead to "an act of giving meaning."[8] Whatever the form taken by these "coalitions of sufferers," they are all based on the same observation: conventional wisdom and traditional politics are helpless when confronted by grief and have nothing to offer sufferers other than the vestiges of a powerless scientism or a bastardized Christianity. Anxious to move beyond both resignation and lament, these broken people gather together so that they do not have to suffer alone. These are minuscule initiatives, sometimes spectacular or sentimental, that seek to reintegrate the sick into the human family and outline a new battle network that is separate from churches, political parties, and institutions.

[8] Daniel Defert, interview with Frédéric Martel, "Face au sida," *Esprit*, July 1994.

Victims or Pioneers?

If it is true that a third power is emerging in civil society, the power of victims,[9] it consists of people who refuse to allow themselves to be reduced to victimhood and who aspire, even in their weakened physical condition, to regain their freedom and responsibility. Rejecting the victimization that argues that a handicap requires special exemptions, they bring their sickness into the public sphere in order to be recognized and to return to normal life: for example, the young French woman aviator who was confined to a wheelchair after an accident and who created a movement to gain acceptance for handicapped pilots. By deciding that a certain abuse is no longer tolerable, and by translating their revolt into legal and political terms, these people modify the norm and shift the threshold of intolerance for everyone. Forced to overcome the indifference of public authorities and the skepticism of medical and psychiatric experts, they have to respond this crucial demand: *prove to me that you are suffering.*[10] Then and only then will they set legal precedents, serve as models for others, and broaden the range of legitimate victims.

A fundamental mutation: because of the demands made on it by hemophiliacs, cancer patients, AIDS patients, and

---

[9] Antoine Garapon and Denis Salas, *La République pénalisée* (Paris: Hachette, 1996), p. 10.

[10] To be accepted, a complaint has to be accompanied by an objective statement by a medical expert and confirmed by a clinical assessment of the symptoms and the degree of pain involved. See Gilles Trimaille, "L'expertise médico-légale: confiscation et traduction de la douleur," in *La Douleur et le Droit*, ed. Poirier, esp. pp. 498–499.

people with disabilities, a whole society is trying to come to terms with a new problem and to take control over its calamities through a dual effort of pragmatism and sheer determination. They are no longer satisfied with what everybody previously accepted. What used to be a matter of bad luck is now conceived in terms of prejudices, that is, a "modifiable inevitability" (Ernst Cassirer). They are fighting, here as elsewhere in the world of work and enterprise, to regain their dignity and to prevent others from defining them exclusively by their disabilities (changing the way people see people with disabilities is the main function of the telethon, which collects funds for research on myopathy). In this way the seriously ill, the traumatized, and accident victims, strong in their common weaknesses, manifest their freedom with regard to what had previously put them in the category of subcitizens, those receiving assistance. They are fighting against the segregation that made them lepers, bearers of bad news. They are fighting to remain members of the human community.[11]

---

[11] In a doctoral dissertation on posttraumatic stress, Dr. Louis Jehel, discussing the fifty-six victims of the terrorist attack in the Port-Royal RER station in Paris on December 3, 1996, shows that women and children are more vulnerable to this kind of dramatic event, and that people who are physically wounded and treated in a hospital recover from stress more quickly. His work pleads for more efficient and rapid assistance to victims of such attacks. Louis Jehel, dissertation, Université de Picardie, Jules-Verne, Faculté de Médecine, November 1997.

Minuscule Revolutions

A philosopher asks: What is the point of marching against AIDS? Who is for AIDS? Do we march against cancer or heart attacks?[12] To this strong objection we must reply that people demonstrate first of all to show how many they are, to recharge their batteries, to act on the symbolic level, and to remind society that we are all concerned. In this domain as in others, the point is to convert the proscribed into honorable victims (and to emphasize that honorable citizens might someday find themselves in the position of the proscribed). Thus Act Up's parades, with posters in the form of obituaries, whistles, and dark clothes, resemble the corteges of pilgrims that passed through cities in the Middle Ages to remind people that they were mortal.[13] Every time modernity is confronted with the essential—that is, with death—it resorts to the religious. *In short, the modern citizen is a suffering subject in revolt against his suffering,* and his revolt can take several forms: a complaint addressed to the welfare state;[14] legal proceedings to gain compensations; and finally, waging a collective or associative battle. It can combine these three forms, but in every case it has

[12] Bertrand Vergely, *La Souffrance* (Paris: Gallimard, 1997).

[13] Whatever else one may think about this organization, which produces provocation the way others produce prose, uses and abuses a revisionist rhetoric (comparing AIDS to the Shoah), demands a Nuremberg trial for this disease, and engages, in the name of the sacredness of the patient raised to the level of a Christ figure, in dubious practices in which it is hard to distinguish publicity seeking from the cause it is defending.

[14] See J. F. Lae, *L'Instance de la plainte. Une histoire politique et juridique de la souffrance* (Paris: Descartes & Cie., 1996).

to choose between a posture of victimhood that puts it under house arrest in its disease and common combat, which forces it to invent new solutions and offer a reasonable outlet for grievances. Either imprisoning oneself in the injury and endless rumination on its dark abjection or reconstructing oneself, which means ceasing to be a martyr and entering the domain of freedom. It is likely that our time will not make a clear decision for either of these two ways of dealing with suffering. But the choice is there. These minuscule revolutions in no way attenuate the distress of the condemned or the loneliness of the dying. *We can cure certain diseases but not disease itself,* which reappears in new forms and perseveres with a diabolic ingenuity that defies our most elaborate resources. Each period, thinking it has supplanted the preceding one, has to bear a new cross. At least our attitude toward pain is changing; it no longer has anything to do with positivist optimism, religious postulates, or hedonistic forgetfulness, which is another form of capitulation. Oscar Wilde wrote, "Those who refuse combat are more seriously injured than those engage in it."

Love Is Not Compassion

It was an immense step forward to raise compassion, "that innate repugnance at seeing a fellow human being suffer" (Rousseau), to the rank of a democratic virtue, a way of seeing humanity as a whole and the animal realm in general, as a single suffering body whose slightest wounds affect us. The domain of law progresses through the horror aroused in us by harm done to others and to our inferior brothers, the animals. Nonetheless, when Rousseau writes in essence: "Every being that suffers is my fellow creature," he clearly extends the feeling of equality and solidarity to all peoples and species, thus putting suffering, and not joy or gaiety, at the center of human experience. Thus we can invert his declaration: only someone who suffers is my fellow creature (and someone who enjoys life is my enemy?).

Let us be wary of the carrion birds who feed on unhappiness and bristle at our prosperity but who, as soon as we are struck by a misfortune, hurry to our bedsides and take pleasure in our distress. Let us be wary of all those who claim to adore the poor, the losers, the excluded. In their solicitude there is a kind of disguised scorn, a way of reducing the wretched to their distress, and never considering them as equals. Under the mask of charity, resentment triumphs: the love of unhappiness, the hatred of people. Others are pardoned for existing only if they suffer.

"To be touched by pity," Cicero said, "implies that one is envious, because if one suffers from other people's misfortunes, one can also suffer from their happiness." Rousseau invented compassion as actual participation in the suffering of others, the sign of creatures' universality. It is high time to oppose to this compassion a codelectation, a coenjoyment, a way of sympathizing with other people's pleasure, instead of tearing them to pieces as soon as they seem better off than we are. Then and only then does the true face of love shine forth: not dubious commiseration, but jubilation at the existence of others. *Delectatio in felicitate alterius*, Leibniz said, I take delight in other people's happiness. There is more nobility of soul in rejoicing in the gaiety of others than in feeling sorry about their misfortunes.

CHAPTER ELEVEN

Impossible Wisdom

There was never yet philosopher that could endure
the toothache patiently.

—SHAKESPEARE, *Much Ado About Nothing*

Death conceals no mystery. It opens no door. It is
the end of a human being.

—NORBERT ELIAS

What is magnificent is that to reassure people, you
have to deny the obvious.

—ROBERT BRESSON

Does Pain Teach Us Something?

We know the famous alternative with which Voltaire confronts us in *Candide*: human beings are born "to live in
the throes of anxiety or the lethargy of boredom." So our
only choice would be between the horror of affliction and
the monotony of peace and quiet. A terrible dilemma! In
reality, our appetite for life requires adversities that we can
cope with, that test our freedom without destroying it. We
need obstacles that we can overcome and that spare us the

double experience of repeated failure and insurmountable suffering. Therein resides the paradox: good things that are obtained without effort have no value (that is why free merchandise attracts us less than it repels us. Even a thief pays a price when he steals other people's property.). To the puerile dream of a life in which the greatest goals would be achieved without effort, we must reply that pleasure dies when the piquancy of resistance evaporates and everything is attained immediately. In order for satisfaction to be complete, we have to take our time, meditate on our plans for a long time, and avoid the haste that spoils the finest impulses. *Let us not call suffering what has to do only with our incompleteness*, let us call it a blessing, a happy surprise, an opportunity to improve ourselves; let us say about it what Plato said about ugliness, that it electrifies us by the repulsion it elicits, whereas beauty puts us to sleep. Every obstacle defeated and surmounted adds to the value of the object in view, and there is a kind of fatigue that we may find repellant but which also produces an unparalleled pleasure. Pain that discourages some people may galvanize others.

Pain is a salutary wake-up call for the body, a vital function that confronts us with our limits and constitutes "the final rampart against madness and death."[1] As we know, the worst illnesses often sneak up on us noiselessly, in "the silence of the organs." Even great questions and decisive turnarounds often result from a defeat that may make it possible to transform confusion into an advan-

---

[1] J. D. Nasio, *Le Livre de la douleur et de l'amour* (Paris: Payot, 1996).

tage, and handicaps into advantages. The whole tragedy of the heir is to find his life masticated and digested before he has even learned to speak, to be tired of everything before he has even tasted it. Because values are not immediately given, and because I am not immediately what I am supposed to be, gaining access to the truth is a chaotic process that presupposes tension and development. Only things that repel us teach us anything; our projects divide the world into a field of activities, and therefore into potential failures and successes. That is why any education, even the most liberal, involves a break, an exit from a state of blessed ignorance, a kind of violence that we inflict on children in order to incorporate them into the dimension of language and duties. In short, a life without combats, without a burden, without effort of any kind, a life that is a straight line instead of a "steep slope" (Xenophon[2]) would be a monument to languor.

But if people attain humanity only through ordeals, we still need to distinguish the latter from penitence. Contrary to the myth according to which one must have greatly suffered in order to know human beings (Elias Canetti is supposed to have told George Steiner that "You will never write great books unless someday you experience a complete mental collapse"), suffering does not teach people anything, it makes them unhappy and bitter. "One has to have very little love for humanity to think that it is by being shattered that a life progresses."[3] In other

---

[2] Quoted in Paul Demon, *L'Idéal de la tranquillité* (Paris: Les Belles-Lettres, 1990), p. 287.

[3] Vergely, *La Souffrance*, p. 71.

words, the only defeats that are beneficial are the ones to which we can give meaning, that lead to broadening and leave us strengthened by an experience that seemed likely to engulf us (in contrast to the Nietzschean aphorism that the media have repeated ad nauseam: whatever doesn't kill me necessarily makes me stronger. I may survive a heart attack or a cancer without ever recovering my earlier health, and without drawing from the experience any wisdom whatever.). What is passionately interesting about the biographies of common or famous people, with their alternating rises, falls, and resurrections, is that they present ordinary individuals capable of showing exceptional courage in desperate situations, of finding a solution.[4] The contemporary hero is a circumstantial hero propelled despite himself beyond the usual norms, an accidental fighter and not a professional brave. In the same way, sports fascinate us because they are a game played against destiny: they emphasize the precariousness of victory and of defeat, constantly calling titles and trophies in question. As an image of the fragility of acquired ranks and honors, sports provide hope for losers and a warning for winners.

Cicero noted that there are soldiers driven by pride and passion who can endure countless sufferings in combat but collapse when struck by a minor illness.[5] We like constraints only when we impose them on ourselves and

---

[4] Discussing children who have been able to overcome immense obstacles and make adult lives for themselves, Boris Cyrulnik points to their *resilience*, a concept that refers to their ability to rebound after suffering a serious blow, but does not automatically designate a special aptitude for happiness. *Un merveilleux malheur* (Paris: Odile Jacob, 1999).

[5] Cicero, *Tusculan Disputations*, bk. 2, chap. 27.

are prepared to expose ourselves to the worst dangers in order to achieve a superior goal (that is why, contrary to what some Eastern religions tell us, we have to rehabilitate the ego, self-esteem, vanity, and narcissism, all excellent things when they work to increase our power). Consider the often inhuman ordeals to which star athletes subject themselves in order to win, whereas the Western world is entirely devoted to the culture of anesthesia. It is for each individual to set the threshold of pain beyond which he refuses to go (what would a life be worth that had never been risked at least once, that had never experienced the intoxicating proximity of death in order to defy it?). The modern project is to combine will and autonomy, so that the inhuman becomes human because I want it and so that I alone establish the scale of pains I am prepared to endure. "Good suffering" is suffering I declare to be necessary for my development, that I can convert into power and knowledge.

We know the example of Rosie Stancer, a British woman explorer who recently made a solo trek to the South Pole to show that she was capable of the feat and to help sick children. Or that of Benoit Lecomte, a Frenchman who swam across the Atlantic to raise money for cancer research as a tribute to his father, who had died of the disease. As if they had wanted to oppose their will to an inevitability, as if the pain they inflicted on themselves somehow compensated for the pain endured by others! A challenge to finitude, a stubborn attempt to push back the body's psychological and physiological limits by subjecting it to a terrible ordeal. These warriors of the useless believe in the laws of symmetry, they think a martyrdom desired and mastered will magically redeem all the others. This morality of endurance that constantly sets new records is above all a morality of conjuration: it reconstitutes the setting of the ignoble, of extreme pain, the better to expel it, and imposes on itself an excess of vexation and dangers in order to exorcise those we encounter every day.

Alas, we cannot choose the blows that life gives us; distress does not strike on command but bursts upon us, especially in the modern, trivial form of catastrophe represented by the accident. Life grows narrower when the proportion of anonymous adversity grows larger than that of freely accepted adversity, when we no longer dare to take risks, to skirt the abyss, for fear of hastening our demise or bringing countless ills upon ourselves. There would be no torment or grief if we could assign a reason and a meaning to all injuries. But we can't, and that is why pain remains unnamable, atrocious, and neither makes us wiser nor teaches us anything. What an illusion in the Stoic practice of *praemeditatio*, the anticipation of future ills the better to avoid them! Thinking that we can make death, illness, or privation easier to bear by preparing for them day and night is a sure way to poison our lives, to spoil the slightest pleasure by imagining its end.[6] A strange

---

[6] "They do not flinch under the blows of fate because they have reckoned with these attacks in advance, because among the things that happen without our wanting them to, even the most painful are alleviated by anticipation, when thought no longer finds anything unexpected in events but dulls the perception of them as if they were old, worn-out things." Philo of Alexandria, 40 CE, quoted in Pierre Hadot, *Qu'est-ce que la philosophie antique* (Paris: Gallimard, 1995), pp. 212–213.

way of granting these scourges full power over us, whereas they are not within our province. How much more lucid is a lack of foresight! It is not true that to live is to prepare ourselves for death and ruin: it is to exhaust all the possibilities life on Earth offers us despite its vicissitudes and its ineluctable end, it is to act as if we were immortal. And we might note that the writer Cioran, who praised suicide in book after book, died of old age and Alzheimer's disease; it is not always easy to bring one's acts into harmony with one's thoughts.

The Magnificent Sufferers

There is nothing more shocking or instructive, in an age drunk on positivity, than to listen to the seriously ill explain why they consider their illness a friend and try to win it over. To put it another way, a few exceptional people find in the horror of sickness an opportunity to explore a new area of existence, and some even find in it a source of joy. I take as evidence for this four contemporary writers who are really our new scandalous figures, our madmen who would have to be pilloried if three of them weren't already dead and the fourth now nearly eighty. The first is Fritz Zorn, a young, middle-class writer from Zurich who has a tumor he describes as "repressed tears":

> I am young, rich, and cultivated; I am unhappy, neurotic, and alone. I come from one of the best families on the right bank of Lake Zurich, also known as

the Golden Shore. I have a middle-class education and I have been well behaved all my life. My family is fairly degenerate, that is probably why I have a problematic heredity and I have been damaged by my surroundings. Naturally, I also have cancer, which might be expected given what I've just said. However, the question of cancer presents itself in two ways: on the one hand it is a bodily disease from which it is very likely I will die before long, though I might also be able to conquer it and survive; on the other hand it is a disease of the soul about which I can say only one thing: I was lucky that it finally manifested itself. I mean by this that with what I've received from my family in the course of my not very pleasant existence, the most intelligent thing I've done is to catch cancer. . . . Since I've been sick, I feel much better than I did before I fell ill.[7]

The writer Hervé Guibert, who has AIDS and wrote about his own death, exclaims: "I'll kiss the hands of the person who'll tell me I'm doomed" and then marvels at the "incredible perspective of intelligence AIDS had brought into my suddenly finite life," concluding that the latter has "something sleek and dazzling in its hideousness," because it "is a very long flight of steps that led assuredly to death, but whose every step represented unique apprenticeship. It was a disease that gave me time to live and its victims time to die, time to discover time, and in the end

[7] Fritz Zorn, *Mars*, trans. Robert and Rita Kimber (New York: Knopf, 1981).

to discover life, so in a way those green monkeys of Africa had provided us with a brilliant modern invention."[8]

Or consider the extraordinary testimony left by Jean-Dominique Bauby, a journalist who suffered, as a result of a brain-stem lesion, from "locked-in syndrome" and was unable to move, speak, or even breathe without assistance, communicating with the world only through blinking his left eye. Transformed into a "scarecrow" and discovering the universe of total paralysis, this man who "seems to have resided in a barrel of dioxin" bursts out laughing: "A strange euphoria then swept over me. Not only was I exiled, paralyzed, mute, half-deaf, deprived of all pleasures and reduced to the life of a jellyfish, but I was also a revolting sight. I was overwhelmed by the kind of nervous laughter that is provoked by multiple catastrophes when, after a final stroke of fate, we finally decide to treat them as a joke."[9]

Finally, this hallucinating report by the English novelist Paul West on his physiological problems. Afflicted by a whole range of calamities, a stroke, atrocious headaches, diabetes, cardiac arrhythmias, skin disorders, and paralysis, he described his illness as "a miraculous accident" that permitted him to attain self-knowledge and opened him to a "biological magic" of which he would otherwise have remained ignorant.

---

[8] Hervé Guibert, *To the Friend Who Did Not Save My Life*, trans. Linda Coverdale (London: Quartet, 1991), pp. 38, 165, 164.

[9] Jean-Dominique Bauby, *Le Scaphandre et le Papillon* (Paris: Robert Laffont, 1997), p. 31. Jean-Jacques Beineix made a splendid documentary about Bauby's case, *L'Alphabet du silence*, presented on the television program "Bouillon de Culture," March 14, 1997.

To be born is to be transformable for better and for worse while awaiting the worst. While observing my body yield to a few of its final dysfunctions, I've succeeded in doing a great deal of work, not always out of defiance, and I sometimes think that this chaotic collapse has inspired me, that is, pushed me beyond the commonplace. I have to be grateful for what has happened to me, for the stimulation and what it has elicited. . . . My great good fortune was to be able to talk and write about my disease, even while suffering from it, unlike others whose illness has destroyed their intellectual capacities along with their bodies. For this aid, *muchas gracias*, even if it was only an accident.[10]

A passionate lover of his own disease, he describes poetically his crises of fibrillation, expresses his astonishment at the effects of each medication, compares surgical procedures to works of art, ultrasound scans to Kandinsky or Dufy, is proud to have come close to dying and almost encountered the Furies, celebrates esoteric medical jargon that brings dead languages, Greek and Latin, fully back to life. Through illness, "a supreme form of art," he has entered, like Fritz Zorn, Jean-Dominique Bauby, and Hervé Guibert, into another reality. Having become a partly bionic being wearing a pacemaker, a "titanium tit," a manmachine made of artifices, he examines his symptoms with "the fervor of a philatelist," draws "a perverse pride" from

---

[10] Paul West, *A Stroke of Genius: Illness and Self-discovery* (New York: Viking, 1995). [*Un accident miraculeux* (Paris: Gallimard, 1998), p. 11.]

what afflicts him, and finds himself "rather exhilarated to have at least had something to say about [his] fate."

Are these provocations, boasts by desperate people strutting the better to conceal their terror? Probably. But why shouldn't we take them seriously, listen to what they're telling us? What is precious in the testimony provided by these writers is that they do away with three canonical attitudes that the West has established for coping with pain: humility, heroism, and revolt. Refusing to adopt the pose of victims or to lapse into religiosity, they elude, through humor, the usual codes of suffering, turn them to their own ends. These ragged beings whose only wealth is a lack try to answer a fundamental question: what can one do when there is nothing more to do, when the body is sinking into the dark? One can still write books, and build in writing a precarious home. Since they have already been defeated, since they "have fallen into the grave for good" (Zorn), they have nothing left to prove, and confess, inappropriately, that they find a certain comfort in the abominable. They form with their illnesses a touchy, amorous couple and feed on what is killing them. Thus they offer a caustic exemplarity, and we are not sure whether it cheers or depresses us. Through this adventure, so inconceivable that it forces them to take up their pens ("It had to happen—it's awful—for my book to see the light of day," Hervé Guibert says), they become in their own way explorers of new human possibilities. "Up to this point, no one has determined what the body can do," Spinoza said. But with the exception of Fritz Zorn, these writers are also creatures of technoscience kept barely alive by medicine, survivors making their way through a double ordeal, existential and chemical. If they attain a kind of paradoxical sublime that excludes neither fear nor self-derision, that is because they transform their impotence into activity and blaze the path to a new domain in which there was previously only terror and opacity.

Having reached a level of horrifying fear, they try to stare down their physical decline, like a nightmare, and defy the monster who is devouring them by consenting to look it in the face. These extremely sick people are experimenters, pioneers camped at the far limits of the species, where the air is almost unbreathable. In their dizzying solitude, they have become mutants who are going away, burning their ships behind them, leaving the shores of the ordinary. What is touching in them is the absence of posing: neither the post-Romantic hodgepodge dear to Thomas Mann and Dostoyevsky, who saw illness as dispensing genius, nor the Nietzschean vision of the superman whom suffering sculpts like a "divine hammer" and purifies. There is no embellishment or pathos: there is nothing to say, that's how it is. These ordinary people speak to us with irony about their desperate situation: the mad provocation of a Fritz Zorn: "Rather cancer than harmony,"[11] the childish theatricality of a Guibert, the stupefying tragedy of marvelous young man transformed

---

[11] It would be a mistake to try to elaborate a new approach to cancer on the basis of Zorn's case, as if the latter were a judgment on society, a protest against intolerable living conditions. Even if Zorn offered, not without grandiloquence, multiple interpretations of his illness, his book tells us nothing about cancer, but a great deal about his hatred of the class to which he belonged.

into a skeleton, an "Auschwitz baby," the desolate narcissism of a Paul West, and especially the silent laughter of a Dominique Bauby are capital. In their reaction, their way of stealing moments of serenity from terror, they are ambassadors for all the patients who are fighting, as they are, against abjectness. Having reached "the extreme of the possible" (Bataille), they spare us facile speeches: since the Nazi death camps, we have known that there comes a point where unhappiness is no longer possible, where sadness and tears have become a useless luxury because one has descended so far into the abyss. Their language, which bears a wound analogous to that of the body, nonetheless unfurls and flourishes as the only thing that will survive them. Cadavers under sentence of death, moving in a high-density atmosphere, they regard their illness from the point of view of someone who is making it a new way of existing amid devastation. Their narratives are not hymns to the glory of man conquering or resisting, but to the glory of man as a poet who is mischievous even in the depth of his debasement, and who transforms, for an instant, his torture into a triumph, an inner adventure. They are mystics, perhaps, but without God, without revelation; and if they experience the joy of thwarting nature one last time, at the moment when it seeks to eliminate them from the world, they do not console us, and they do not teach us anything. Maybe we read them to conjure the curse that has struck them; but we also read them to see that a death without hope of a beyond, of a reincarnation, is possible. Expropriated of themselves, these mocking Stoics address a final farewell to us before being engulfed. They do not cure us of the obsessive terrors of the night; they project onto its shadows a thin ray of light. They put words to new sufferings, and that is what disturbs us: these astronauts of inner space speak to us from a distant planet that is already our own and on which they are the first to tread.

Temporary Armistices

Finally, let us forestall a misinterpretation: among us there is not, and probably will never be again, the kind of wisdom with regard to suffering that existed among the ancients, and that still exists among Buddhists, for the simple reason that wisdom presupposes a balance between the individual and the world and this balance has long since been lost, at least since the beginning of the Industrial Revolution. We bow our heads before sickness and aging, but this very temporary docility will be abandoned as soon as human ingenuity makes it possible to change previously accepted norms. (And science is really our last adventure, our last great narrative, the bearer of dreams as well as nightmares, and it alone is capable of combining poetry, action, and utopia.)

How sad it is, for example, to think that one is going to die of a disease, a virus that will be curable in a few years, that one is leaving too early (and we know the inverse case of AIDS patients who, thanks to tritherapy, have had to say farewell to their final farewell and rejoin the living). *Pain is a fact, we don't need to make a religion out of it*, and we can make only temporary armistices with the inevitable.

We have seen so many ills disappear that we cannot resign ourselves to suffering the ones that we still have to
endure. Although "human powers stop at the gates of
death" (Aristotle), we can keep those gates closed as long
as possible (and we know that in this domain research is
advancing by leaps and bounds). There is in the world a
great impatience with misfortune and suffering, because
the progress already realized makes the immensity of what
remains to be done odious. The "bestiality" of distress
(Pavese) prevents us from establishing proper relationships
with it other than chaotic and uneven ones. Any serenity in
this matter would be merely the result of fatigue.

If we can only admire the new culture of caring for the
dying that is developing in the West and that spares the
dying the terrible burden of solitude and pain by bear-
ing them "as if on a good ship toward the dark night"
(Marie de Hennezel), we cannot for all that discern in it
the beginnings of a new art of dying, if one ever existed.
Let us beware of the lyricism of the Grim Reaper who
transforms the death of others into an idyllic romance. In
some propagandists for palliative care, we find a kind of
intoxication that leads them to euphemize everything, to
give us a rosy depiction of a tragic event. These *converts
to a cheerful death agony* sometimes show, behind their
kindness, a fanaticism that is frightening, especially when
it leads them to refuse, to those who ask for it, help in
hastening the end, on the pretext that the death agony is
a moment of truth of which no one should be deprived.
(In this respect we still do not have a statute on the dying,

which Philippe Ariès called for more than thirty years ago, especially regarding euthanasia, which is still prohibited in France although it is frequently practiced in a clandestine and "administrative" way.[12])

Even if there is something scandalous about the modern cover-up of death—for example, there are virtual cemeteries on the Internet where you can watch a relative's or friend's funeral on your computer screen—must we transfigure death into a miraculous event and describe other people's deaths as moments of joy—at the risk of slipping into a kind of will to power exerted on exhausted people to whom we attribute positive feelings?

Perhaps the point of this exercise in funereal ventriloquism is to use the dying to reassure ourselves that death is not so serious, to immunize ourselves against it by greedily contemplating other people's deaths? These implacable lovers of last moments sometimes have inexplicable bursts of joy when patients expire,[13] as if the latter, perched on a crest where a whole destiny is collected, had become inter-

[12] As Jacques Pohier clearly explains, in cases of extreme physical decline, the choice is no longer between life and death but between two forms of death. The body is already falling to pieces, but therapeutic obstinacy keeps it artificially alive. See Pohier, *La Mort opportune* (Paris: Seuil, 1998). On the same subject, see the very complete overview provided by Anita Hocquard, *L'Euthanasie volontaire* (Paris: PUF, 1999).

[13] "After leaving Danièle [a person whose life was coming to an end] I felt a desire to run barefoot through the grass, like a madwoman. To get drunk on movement. I drove to the park in Sceaux. . . . On the lawn in front of the chateau, I took an immense pleasure in running, spinning around, feeling the warm, damp earth. I thanked life and Danièle for this intense moment of conscious pleasure." Marie de Hennezel, *La Mort intime* (Paris: Laffont, 1995), pp. 161–162.

mediaries, professors of truth who have glimpsed the light and are going to give us tips about the beyond.[14] Apart from the fact that the idea of providing support for those who are suffering is in principle a dubious idea because one is "always late for the meeting with the neighbor" (Catherine Challier), death, we can talk about it all we want to because no one knows what happens to us afterward. Religions, Kierkegaard said, are travel agencies that promise us a guaranteed ticket to heaven, but no one has ever come back to say whether he was satisfied with the transportation and lodging. The sole form of survival we are certain about is that of the memory we leave in those close to us, and that is the only precarious immortality of which mortals can be sure. The rest is pure speculation. All beliefs are respectable, but it is to beg the question to make death the door to a better world, to turn the great unhappy event into a happy one (which is another form of denial). With regard to death, Jankélévitch said more modestly, there is neither victory nor defeat because it is not an adversary one can vanquish or domesticate. But the friends of the Grim Reaper, those lovers of the moribund, give the impression that they hold the viaticum, the solution for the final instants converted in every case into a happy end. In their credo there is a hatred of

---

[14] Thus in the work of Elizabeth Kübler-Ross, an American pioneer in palliative care, a rather embarrassing eulogy for the seriously ill and especially for AIDS, conceived as a collective accelerator of our humanization, an apparent evil which is in reality a profound good. When this physician tells us in her memoirs that she has direct dialogue with Jesus, daily conversations with ghosts, and thinks of death as a haven of peace, we have left the domain of ideas and entered the unfathomable domain of phantasmagoria.

life, a dreadful gluttony for misfortune that reminds us of the darkest pages in the history of Christianity. In any case, how bizarre to argue that grief, sorrow, and incurable diseases are enrichments! Even if a few individuals can make that claim on a strictly personal basis, like the four authors previously mentioned, it becomes intolerable as soon as it is generalized. What we are experiencing is not a revolution in dying but a new consideration of the dying as living persons with full rights, and that is already very important.

Although we have to cure ourselves of the desire to cure everything and to free human beings from their fragility and imperfection, it would be absurd to demand that we yield to the Minotaur of suffering and resign ourselves to our limits on the ground that the human race is not indefinitely malleable. *The fact that not everything is possible does not mean that nothing is permitted.* And the borderline between insurmountable inevitabilities and modifiable injustices is no sooner established than it has already shifted. We cannot do everything, but we can intervene in the domains that depend on us, we can ally ourselves with "nature" to combat it when it tries to eliminate us. That is the pragmatic attitude of our societies which, since they do not have the key to human distress, undertake therapeutic makeshifts, temporary solidarities, thereby combining humility with determination. We are free to loosen our bonds, but not to free ourselves from them forever, and we set limits only to transgress them. It is for each generation to continue the combat where the preceding one left off, knowing full well that every advance leads to new regressions, that the elimination of one scourge is immediately followed by the emergence of a new one. This war opens up as many battles as it ends. We have never fought so much against the calamities of life as we have since we have discovered that there is no permanent solution for our misfortunes. Thus suffering comes back, but in a different place, not as an inevitability or a vestige but as an inseparable double that is intertwined with our lives and that we try to expel even if we see that the struggle has no end.

What we are awkwardly groping toward today is an art of living that includes an acknowledgment of adversity but does not fall into the abyss of renunciation: an art of enduring that allows us to exist with suffering and against it.

Success for Buddhism in the West?

Everything is suffering: being born is suffering, getting old is suffering, sickness is suffering, being bound to what we do not like is suffering, being separated from what we love is suffering. To escape this curse, we have to learn to detach ourselves from the world, to kill desire in us, to escape the cycle of reincarnations or at least find a way of being born into a better fate. The reader will have recognized, crudely summarized in these lines, one of the foundations of Buddhism. It is astonishing that this doctrine, which makes the self a harmful illusion, has gained so much influence in the hedonistic and individualistic West.

What is peculiar about Buddhism in relation to our monotheistic religions is that it is not dogmatic and issues no commands, but rather indicates a way to escape from restless wandering and invites each person to find the path that leads to salvation. Above all, it re-creates a link, which has long since disappeared in the West, between theory and practice: unlike the Western philosopher, who is pure spirit devoted to speculation, the Buddhist teacher, like the ancient teacher, is first of all a teacher of life. He proposes no ideas that he has not tried out, and his teaching takes its nourishment from the living source of experience. And there is more: by calling on us to extinguish the ardor of our thirst, to renounce desires, Buddhism joins and reawakens one of the central axioms of Christianity: the ephemeral, empty character of our life on Earth. Again like Christianity, Buddhism considers suffering a way of cleansing the individual of bad karma, that is, of atoning for the sins committed in an earlier life. Like Christianity, it draws its prestige from being situated outside life. In short, it seems to have succeeded where our churches have failed: as a counterweight restraining the appetite for wealth and excessive egoism. Its attraction seems to derive from its proximity and not from its distance, and from its very rich cultural tradition. It seems that truths we no longer tolerate when expressed by our own religions we can hear when they are expressed under an Asian mask.

However, it is not at all clear that this is so. Except for a very small number of scholars and literary people, what has triumphed in the West is not Buddhism but a pick-and-choose religion decked out with exoticism. It is not even a form of spirituality, it is a therapy, a shield against stress that promulgates an all-purpose credo acceptable to the masses. How can a doctrine of renunciation seduce a society so implicated in the world? By renouncing renunciation, by serving it up in a "lite" form digestible by our delicate stomachs, by our supercharged egos. Then we can dig around in it as if it were a box of chocolates, picking out the best pieces and rejecting the others. What matters is that the packaging remain Tibetan, Zen, or Tantric.

In this infatuation with Asia, something else may be involved: the invention of an unprecedented syncretism, a magical reconciliation of contraries, of serenity and uneasiness, of attachment and indifference, of personal development and the illusion of the self, by way of a minimal belief. What is this neo-Buddhism? The spiritual counterpart of a spiritless globalization, the religion of the end of religions? Maybe. From this mad embrace of East and West, which is contemporary with the era of facile doctrines, something will emerge that is unlike anything we know: certainly not authentic Buddhism, which is still too rigid, too disciplined, and will be disfigured, trampled upon, the victim of its own success. What will emerge is a gigantic misinterpretation, the eternal form of novelty in history.

Madame Verdurin's Croissant

Believe those who seek the truth,
doubt those who find it.

—ANDRÉ GIDE

When in 1915 Madame Verdurin learns of the loss of the *Lusitania*, a British ocean liner sunk by a German submarine, she is enjoying her first croissant of the war. The abrupt arrival of this news in no way lessens her pleasure in rediscovering a taste so familiar:

> Mme Verdurin, who suffered from headaches on account of being unable to get croissants to dip into her coffee, had obtained an order from Cottard which enabled her to have them made in the restaurant mentioned earlier. It had been almost as difficult to procure this order from the authorities as the nomination of a general. She started her first croissant again on the morning the papers announced the wreck of the *Lusitania*. Dipping it into her coffee, she arranged her newspaper so that it would stay open without her having to deprive her other hand of its function of dipping, and exclaimed with horror, "How awful! It's more frightful than the most

terrible tragedies." But those drowning people must have seemed to her reduced a thousand-fold, for, while she indulged in these saddening reflections, she was filling her mouth and the expression on her face, induced, one supposes, by the savor of the croissant, a precious remedy for her headache, was rather that of placid satisfaction.[1]

Is Madame Verdurin a hypocrite? Not at all. She is simply human, terribly human, and we must not allow ourselves to be misled by Proust's irony here. We are never so happy as amid others' distress, when we are temporarily freed from our cares and from the grave concern that furrows people's foreheads. We laugh and love at the same time that millions of people are suffering and dying, just as at the hour of our death, our suffering, millions of people who don't know or love us will be amusing themselves and playing. We are all Madame Verdurins in this regard, for the different parts of humanity live in different time frames, even within a particular group: the sight of our friends' joy when we are enduring sorrow or grief can wound us like an insult. And the instantaneous broadcast of news around the world changes nothing: seeing a famine on the eight o'clock news has never prevented anyone from enjoying a good meal.

Let us be wary of the common but false notion that our happiness depends on that of others and by extension on that of society as a whole. Here we have to shift to a

[1] Marcel Proust, À la Recherche du temps perdu (Paris: Gallimard/Pléiade, 1954), 3: 772–773. Translation by C. K. Scott-Moncrieff.

different scale: we do not live in isolation but in limited groups—families, friends, towns, regions—that determine our moods and our pleasures. We are defined, Hume said, not by universality but by partiality,[2] a combination of sympathy and egoism, a very particular angle on life that is all the more imperious because it is unaware of itself. Our gloomy or gay view of things is often conditioned by this narrow environment that influences us as much as we influence it. Thus there is a happiness that is elicited by others but whose scope is limited to a few intimates and never radiates to the ends of the earth. The ideal would be, of course, to reconcile personal and collective pleasure, and to realize oneself in a world in which all oppression and poverty had been eliminated. It is true that each joyful moment includes an implicit desire to improve humanity, to share this delight with everyone. But if injustices had to be wiped out in order to achieve "nirvana," we would not be able to manage even a faint smile. Horror and abomination surround us, but we go on living and prosper, and we are right to do so because this insensitivity is indispensable for keeping our balance. Regardless of the point of view taken, there is no happiness save in insouciance, unconsciousness, and innocence, in the rare moments stolen from uneasiness and alarm. We are happy only in spite: in spite of a friend who is suffering, of a war that is killing people, of a sick universe, and there is no shame in being happy because there will always be calamities and

[2] Quoted by Philippe Raynaud in *Politesse et sincérité* (Paris: Éditions Esprit, 1984), p. 85.

massacres that indefinitely postpone the perfect social condition.

However, this implies a consequence: because it is the expression of a saving detachment, because it claims to escape the evil spells of time and stop change in its tracks, happiness cannot be the ultimate goal of human societies or the basis for action. Like suffering, it has to be subordinated to freedom. These moments of coincidence with oneself and harmony with nature, these luminous pages that transfigure our existence, cannot provide us with the foundation for a morality, a politics, or a project. If we must teach people to resist their inclinations, that is because not all goals are compatible; we have to prioritize them, and even abandon some that are dear to us. There are circumstances in which freedom may prove more important than happiness, sacrifice more important than tranquility. Condorcet's characteristic idea of an "indissoluble linkage" between virtue, justice, reason, and pleasure is not tenable. Even if we can postulate that all goods are connected through the unity of a life (Charles Taylor), they necessarily conflict as soon as we try to realize them. That is why politics belongs to the order of prudence, not that of the sublime, and that is why history remains tragic and stains us all, no matter what our personal commitments may be. The simultaneous flourishing of human ideals is a delightful dream, but fragmentation is our fate; we are doomed to dissonance and to the competition between ultimate values that turn out to be irreconcilable.

Finally, it is perhaps time to say that the "secret" of a good life is not to give a damn about happiness: never to seek it as such, to accept it without asking whether it is deserved or contributes to the edification of the human race; not to cling to it, not to regret its loss; to let it retain its fantastic character, which allows it to emerge in the middle of ordinary days or to slip away in grandiose situations. In short, we have to consider it always and everywhere secondary since it never occurs except in relation to something else.

To happiness in the strict sense, we may prefer pleasure, as a brief moment of ecstasy stolen in the course of things, gaiety, the lighthearted drunkenness that accompanies life's development, and especially joy, which presupposes surprise and elation. For nothing can compete with the irruption in our lives of an event or a being that ravages and ravishes us. There is always too much to desire, to discover, to love. And we leave the stage having hardly tasted the feast.

INDEX

accident, 211
acedia, 85–86
Act Up, 203, 203n13
adversity, as human need, 206–208
advertising, 47–48, 173
AIDS, 213–214, 219; societal response to, 198–200
Alain (Émile-Auguste Chartier), 57; *Propos sur le bonheur*, 42, 184
Alcoholics Anonymous, 197–198
Almodóvar, Pedro, 158
Americans, as utilitarians, 75
American way of life, in work of Fitzgerald, 168–169
Amiel, Henri-Frédéric, 87–90, 92–93, 120
ancients, and refutation of suffering, 185–186, 186n2, 219
anesthesia, culture of, 210
animal rights, 190
anteriority, principle of, 147
antibourgeois sentiment, 131–136, 140–143, 145–146
anticapitalist sentiment, 145–146
anxiety, over health, 52–55
Aquinas, St. Thomas, 11, 86
Aragon, Louis, *Paysan de Paris*, 118n5
Arendt, Hannah, 132
Ariès, Philippe, 184, 187, 221

Aristotle, 6, 149–150, 171, 178, 220
armistices, temporary, with suffering, 219–224
artist, bourgeois as, 142
art of enduring, 224
art of living, 224
ascesis, 90
athletes, 210
Attali, Jacques, 146
Aubenque, Pierre, 82n3
Augustine of Hippo, St., 3, 10, 12, 18, 71; *Confessions*, 86
Auschwitz, 22, 139, 139n10
automatic writing, 119
autonomy, and will, 210

Bacon, Francis, *New Atlantis*, 28
bad luck, 61–62
bad taste. *See* vulgarity
Balzac, Honoré de, *L'Histoire des Treize*, 116
banality, 4, 165–166; abolition of, 115–120; birth of, 70–74; embrace of, 87–90; martyrs of, 84–86; and repetitiveness of everyday life, 76–83; and secularism, 69–70. *See also* boredom
baptism, of newborn, 20
bàraka, 105
Barthes, Roland, 95
Bataille, Georges, 218

Bauby, Jean-Dominique, 214, 218
Baudelaire, Charles, 77–78
Baudrillard, Jean, 55
beatitudes, in Gospels, 25
beauty, rich people as models of, 164
"be happy." *See* duty to be happy
Beineix, Jean-Jacques, *L'Alphabet du silence,* 214n9
Bell, Daniel, 140
Bénichou, Paul, 29
Bentham, Jeremy, 28
Berlin, Isaiah, 66
Bible: Gospel of Luke, 25n21; Gospel of Matthew, 12, 14, 25n21
Birot, Pierre-Albert, 120
Bloch, Ernst, 27n1
body, human: and "fun," 91–92; reconciliation with, 29–30. *See also* health; illness; pain; suffering
bodybuilding, 55
bonfires of the vanities, 9–10
boredom, 37–38; and horror in wartime, 139; metaphors of, 77; and monastic life, 84–86; virtues of, 125–126; of working people, 165
Bossuet, Jacques-Bénigne, 11–12, 14, 24
Bourdieu, Pierre, 140
bourgeois gentleman (Molière), 151
bourgeoisie, 131–136, 185; and guilty conscience, 140–142; triumph of, 142–146; and vulgarity, 153–156
Brassaï (Gyula Halasz), 108
Breton, André, 27n1, 115–116
Buddhism: and solution by dissolution, 194; and suffering,

23, 219; in the West, 59–61, 224–226
Bunyan, John, *Pilgrim's Progress,* 70
Burroughs, William, 175
Butler, Samuel, *Erewhon,* 183–184

calendar, as constraint, 120–121
Campanella, Tommaso, 29
Camus, Albert, 27n1, 46
cancer, 212–213, 217n11
Canetti, Elias, 208
Canguilhem, Georges, 99n6
capitalism, and consumerism, 40. *See also* bourgeoisie
carpe diem, 110
Carrière, Jean-Claude, 56n11
Carroll, Lewis (C. L. Dodgson), 109
Cassirer, Ernst, 202
Catholic Church: and attraction to suffering, 21–22; and Christian death, 24; and eschatological texts, 34; and indulgences, 16n8; and invention of purgatory, 15–16; and norm of suffering, 22–23
Cazeneuve, Jean, 59n16
celebrities, cult of, 178–179
celebrity magazines, 178
cell phone, 80
Cerroli, 79
Challier, Catherine, 222
charity, and resentment, 205
Chekhov, Anton, 135–136
Chesterton, G. K., 38
Chopra, Deepak, 60, 60n17
Christian art, and suffering, 22
Christian calculus, 14
Christianity: and hope of salvation, 33; and renunciation of

the world, 225; and suffering, 20–26, 35, 186; views on happiness, 9–18. *See also* Catholic Church; Orthodox Church; Protestantism; Reformation
Christmas every day, 115–116
Cicero, Marcus Tullius, 64, 205; *Tusculan Disputations*, 186n2, 209
Cioran, Emil, 212
citizen, as suffering subject in revolt against his suffering, 203–204
class differences, in bourgeoisie, 142–143
Club of Rome, 145n14
coalitions of sufferers, 197–200
Cobain, Kurt, 81
Coella, Rosolino, 79
coenjoyment, of happiness of others, 205
coercion, charitable, 48–51
collective action, against suffering, 203–204
comfort, 30, 165
common people: happiness of, 122–124; and vulgarity, 149–151
communism, fall of, 33
compassion, distinct from love, 204–205
competition, social, 173–174
Conche, Marcel, 23n18
Condorcet, Nicolas de (Marie-Jean-Antoine-Nicolas de Caritat, marquis de Condorcet), 31, 230
conformism, 4; among the rich, 166–167
Congrès de Banalyse, 90
connection, human, through

shared ordeal, 197–200
conservatives, political, 141
consolation by comparison, 111–112
conspicuous consumption, 173
conspiracy of silence, concerning misfortune, 185–186
Constant, Benjamin, 46
consumerism, 40–41, 47–48, 173
contentment, 114–115
contrast, need for, 118
culminations, mystique of, 115–120
Curie, Marie, 42
customary society, 75
Cutler, Howard, 56n12, 56n14
Cyrulnik, Boris, 209n4

Dalai Lama, 51n9, 56n11–56n12, 56n14, 59–61
Dante Alighieri, 73
death: absurdity of, 188; Christian, 23–24; defied by pleasure, 45; everpresent nature of, 13; fear of, 185; preparation for, 211–212; prohibition of, 184; public, in early modern period, 23–24; and sex, 199; and survival, 222; three types of, 13–14; and youth, 199
Debord, Guy, 117
Declaration of Independence, 30
de Maistre, Joseph, 132
democracy: and banality, 72–74; and vulgarity, 157
depression: and *acedia*, 86; as response to happiness imperative, 48–51
de Quincey, Thomas, 58
Descartes, René, 13–14

Deschiens, Les (French TV show), 158
desire, insatiable, 175
destiny, bourgeoisie and, 134–136
detective novel, 103–104
Diagnostic and Statistical Manual of Mental Disorders (DSM), 95, 95n5
diarists, 87–90
Diderot, Denis, 3
Dionysius Areopagiticus, 34
disability rights, 201–202
discretion, 112–113
diseases, 101; persistence of, 204
divine unreason, 124–126
doctors, and patients, 195–197
Dostoyevsky, Fyodor, 217
Drieu La Rochelle, Pierre, 98, 138
drugs, 57–58; pain-relieving, 25
Duchamp, Marcel, 119
Dumézil, Georges, 10
Dupont de Nemours, Pierre Samuel, 29
duty to be happy, 1–3, 5, 40–51; origin of phrase, 42n2
dying, caring for, 220–224
dysfunctional persons, 58

economy, as religion, 143–146
Eden: and idea of progress, 31–35; as locus of happiness, 10–11
education: as form of persecution, 191; through pain, 206–212
Ehrenberg, Alain, 59n16
elitism, and vulgarity, 160
Éluard, Paul, 27n1
emulation, 114–115
Encyclopédie, 124
endurance, morality of, 208–211

Enlightenment, 38, 72; and the bourgeoisie, 131–136; on compatibility of virtue and pleasure, 45; and idea of progress, 35; and promise of happiness, 27–31; and pursuit of happiness, 1–3, 5; and rehabilitation of pleasure, 26; and suffering, 33
environmental influences, 229
envy, 4, 111–115, 165–167
Epictetus, 21, 186n2, 194
Epicureans, and suffering, 21
Epicurus, 184, 186n2
eternal present, everyday life as, 76–83
ethic of seeming to feel good about oneself, 50–51
Europeans, and *savoir-vivre,* 75
euthanasia, 221
everyday life: Amiel and, 87–90; as frenetic inertia, 76–83; transfiguration of, 115–120. *See also* banality
evil, persistence of, 35–38. *See also* suffering
exceptional, invisible, 120
exclusivity of the rich, 166–167
existentialism, 46
exoticism, 167, 225
exteriority principle, 109, 147–148

failure, lifelong, 61–62
fantastic literature, 103–104
fast food, 75
fatalism, 97–98
fatigue: abstract, 79–80; in monastic life, 85–86
fear: and missed opportunity, 108; pleasure of, in safety, 103–104; in wartime, 139

festive ideology, 127–128
festivity, two states of, 127–128
fiction, literary, 103–104
Fitzgerald, F. Scott, 168–169
Flaubert, Gustave, 77, 109, 135,
   159–160
form, in life and art, 81–82
Fourier, Charles, 48
France: contemporary, 175; Old
   Regime, 132–133, 150; Second
   Empire, 151, 160; Third Republic,
   184; twentieth-century, 177
freedom not to be happy, 66
French Revolution, 28, 31, 36
frenetic inertia, 76–83
Freud, Sigmund, 195; *Civilization
   and Its Discontents,* 39–40; on
   Dostoyevsky, 15n5
Freudianism, and introspection,
   100
frugality, morality of, 174–177
fun, utopia of, 91–92
Furet, François, 141
future, as locus of hope, 30

Garden Gnome Liberation Front,
   159
gardening, 122–124
gastronomy, 75
Gautier, Théophile, 136
genocide, use of term, 193
Getty, J. Paul, 174
Gide, André: *Nourritures terrestres,*
   43; *Nouvelles nourritures,* 43
God, goodness of, and existence
   of evil, 23
Goethe, Johann Wolfgang von, 78
Gogol, Nikolai, 134
goodness of God, and existence of
   evil, 23

"good suffering," 206–212. *See also*
   suffering
greeting, as minimal social bond,
   18–19
Groddeck, Georg, 45
Gross National Happiness
   (GNH), 145
Guibert, Hervé, 213–214, 216–217
Guilloux, Louis, 81

habits, transfiguration of, 74–75
happiness: as abstraction, 4, 172–
   174; arbitrariness of, 124–126; as
   art of the indirect, 51; blindness
   of, 187; bourgeois, 138–139; as
   Christian theme, 25–26; conflated with comfort, 143–146;
   as curse, 62–66; dependent on
   that of others, 228–230; economy of, 37–38; and the everyday,
   78; found in writing, 82, 216;
   health as, 52–55; impossibility
   of, 39–40; inevitability of, 31; as
   injunction, 1–3, 5, 40–51; inner
   conviction of, 113; "in spite of,"
   229–230; literature of, 147; located in past or future, 10–11; of
   mass public, 122–124; mistaken
   notions of, 5–6; nonlife as,
   87–90; as norm, 65–66; of others, 111–115; and others' distress,
   227–228; paradoxes of, 3–5; as
   permanent state, 115–120, 153;
   postponement of, 184–187;
   promise of, 27–31; and quest
   for salvation, 12–14; as reward
   of existence, 190; and role of
   grace, 62–63; of some, as kitsch
   of others, 160; subordinated to
   freedom, 230; theories of, 3;

happiness *(continued)*
  voluntary nature of, 41–47; as
  word, 44–45
"happiness gene," 152–153
health: as happiness, 52–55; as lack
  of concern about self, 54; obsessive pursuit of, 52–61
heaven, as locus of happiness,
  10–11. *See also* paradise
hedonism: as absolute value, 188;
  linked to failure and disgrace,
  64–66
Hegel, G.W.F., 26, 32, 71
Heine, Heinrich, 27n1
hell, as Renaissance invention, 15
Hennezel, Marie de, 220, 221n13
Henriette Anne d'Angleterre,
  Duchess of Orléans, 24
heretics, and hope, 25–26
hero and heroism, 21, 90, 209, 216
Hitler, Adolf, 137
homosexuality, 142n12
hope, biblical inspiration for,
  25–26
hospice care, 220–224
"how's it going?" as formula of
  greeting, 18–19
Huizinga, Johan, 29, 70
human suffering. *See* suffering
humility, as response to pain, 216
Huxley, Aldous, *Brave New
  World,* 57
"hyperclass," transnational, 146
hypochondriacs, 58, 101, 196

identity politics, 141–142
illness, 98–103. *See also* pain;
  suffering
imitation, and vulgarity, 153–156
immigrants, and physical labor, 191

incarnation, doctrine of, 17
individual, autonomous, 40,
  43–47
indulgences, 16n8
inertia, frenetic, 76–83
inheritance, 176, 176n5
innovation, and vulgarity, 156
insouciance, 229–231; loss of,
  52–61
Internet, 51, 76, 175
introspection, Freudianism and,
  100

James, Henry, "The Beast in the
  Jungle," 106–107
Jankélévitch, V., 65, 86, 222
Jaspers, Karl, 138
Jehel, Dr. Louis, 202n11
John Cassian, St., *Institutes of the
  Coenobia,* 85n1
John Paul II, pope, 20, 96; on
  euthanasia, 24; on suffering,
  22–23
joie de vivre, 122–124, 122n8
Jünger, Ernst, 138

Kant, Immanuel, 30–31, 42n2,
  120, 150
Kierkegaard, Søren, 222
kitsch, aesthetics of, 158–159
Kolakowski, Leszek, 171
Koons, Jeff, 158
Kübler-Ross, Elizabeth, 222n14

language, corruption of, 193
Lassalle, Ferdinand, 123
Lecomte, Benoit, 210
legal profession, and proliferation
  of suffering, 191
Leibniz, Gottfried, 205

Leriche, René, 54
Leroux, Pierre, 27n1
Levine, Mark, 176n5
liberal democracies, and denial of suffering, 185–188
liberation of mores, 139–140
life: inspiring, 148; of perpetual failure, 61–62; successful, 161–162; well failed, 161–162
Lilla, Mark, 140n11
Locke, John, 28
locked-in syndrome, 214
loneliness, fear of, 185
longevity, pursuit of, 52–55, 58–59
lost illusions, 147–148
love: distinct from compassion, 204–205; distinct from happiness, 194
luck, 112. *See also* bad luck
Lucretius (Titus Lucretius Carus), 112
Luther, Martin, 12, 16–17
Luxemburg, Rosa, 123
luxury, 177

magazines, 90; and happiness imperative, 63–64
"magnificent sufferers," 212–219
Malebranche, Nicolas, 17, 42n2
Mallarmé, Stéphane, 77
Mann, Thomas, 217
manners: formalism of, 157–158; rich people as models of, 164
Marcuse, Herbert, 45
marginal, attraction of, 167
Marx, Karl, 26, 32
massacres, of late twentieth century, 171–172
May 1968, events of, 43–45
meaning, and happiness, 124–126

media, and celebrity, 178–179
medicalization of life, 52–55
medical omnipotence, myth of, 199
medical specialization, 196–197
melatonin, 57, 57n15
Men's Health magazine, 64n19
menuaille, 134
meteorology, 92–98
Middle Ages, 151
middle classes, 149–150, 150n1; American, 176n4
millenarians, and hope, 25–26
Miller, Henry, 44
millionaires, 165, 165n2
minorities, as trendsetters, 167
Mirabeau (Honoré Gabriel Riqueti, comte de Mirabeau), plan for happiness, 1–3
misfortune: and conspiracy of silence, 185–186; expansion of concept, 191–192; negation of, 183–184; renewed recognition of, 193–195
misfortunes, enumeration of, 184–185
Misrahi, Robert, 125
missed opportunities, 106–111
Mitterrand, François, 189
modern art, and transfiguration of the commonplace, 119–120
modernity: and banality, 70–71; and nostalgia/remorse, 38; and self-hatred, 146; and vulgarity, 156–160
Molière (Jean-Baptiste Poquelin), 151
monastic life, and boredom, 84–86
money: as abstraction, 172–174; hierarchy of, 170–171; as "necessary immorality," 170; our

money (continued)
 relationship to, 174–175; veneration of, 143–146; and vulgarity,
 154–156
Montaigne, Michel Eyquem de,
 195
Montesquieu (Charles-Louis de
 Secondat, baron de Montesquieu), 133
moods, linked to weather, 92–98
morality, of endurance, 208–211
Morand, Paul, 71
Moravia, Alberto, 77
More, Sir Thomas, 29
mourning, and repression of
 tears/grief, 187
mystery, notion of, 23, 23n18
mystics, Christian, and aesthetics
 of torture and blood, 22

Nasio, J. D., 207
natural catastrophes, and human
 negligence, 97–98
natural law, and moral imperative, 45
Nazi death camps, 218. See also
 Auschwitz
Nazism, 124, 132, 138
negligence, human, and natural
 catastrophes, 97–98
negotiation, and concept of purgatory, 15–16
neo-Buddhism, 224–226
neoliberalism, 140
neuropharmacology, 152–153
newborn: baptism of, 20; suffering of, 32–33
Nietzsche, Friedrich, 26, 80,
 122n8, 173, 194
nightclubs, 127

Nizan, Paul, 136
North Africa, French returned
 from, 155n4
nostalgia, of modernity, 38
nouveau riche, 154–156

old age, 99–100
original sin, 20, 36; everyday life
 as, 117
Orthodox Church, and attraction
 to suffering, 21–22
Other, our suffering for and
 because of, 194
others, as prompters, 114–115
Ouaki, 56n13
overwork, 165

pain: changing attitude toward,
 204; distinct from penitence,
 208–211; as fact, not religion,
 219; "lessons" of, 206–212;
 persistence of, 35–38. See also
 suffering
pain relief, and notion of suffering, 25
palliative care, 220–224
paradise: and idea of progress,
 31–35; representations of, 33–34
paradoxes, of being happy, 3–5
Park, Andrew, 115–116
Pascal, Blaise, 35; on death, 13, 24;
 on Epictetus, 21; on happiness
 before the Fall, 10; on hope of
 redemption, 12, 14; Pensées, 94
Passion, of Christ, 20
patient: confronting his illness,
 200, 212–219; as educator of
 others, 200
patients, and doctors, 195–197
patronage, 170

Pavese, Cesare, 220
Péguy, Charles, 132
Pelagian heresy, 35
penalism, 97–98
penitence, Christian, 15
perfectibility, belief in, 28
Philo of Alexandria, 211n6
physical effort, as misfortune, 191
Pinçon, Michel, 166n3
Pinçon-Charlot, Monique, 166n3
Pinoncelli, Pierre, 119n7
pioneers, patients as, 212–219
Plato: *Republic*, 150; on ugliness, 207
pleasure: compatibility with virtue, 45; and defiance of death, 45; insufficiency of, 48–51; perpetual, 115–120; preferred to happiness, 231; rehabilitation of, 29. *See also* fun
pleasures, small, 122–124
Poe, Edgar Allen, 77, 103
Pohier, Jacques, 221n12
Pollan, Stephen, 176n5
pop art, 159
Portier, Louis, 196
possibilities, 109–111
poverty, 176; in developed countries, 171; involuntary, 170, 177; in United States, 176n4; voluntary, 177
praemeditatio, 211
prayers, answered, 147–148
productivist logic, and pleasure, 117
progress, idea of, 30–31; as defense of present suffering in name of future improvement, 31–33; and notion of paradise, 31–35; and realization of happiness, 34–35

proletariat, decline of, 142
prompters, others as, 114–115
prosperity, 143–146
prostitution, 117–118
Protestantism, 143; and attraction to suffering, 21–22
Proust, Marcel, 108, 163; *À la Recherche du temps perdu*, 227–228
provinces, concept of, 77–78
pseudo-Dionysius the Areopagite, 34
punctuality, 120–121
purgatory, 15–16, 16n8

Racine, Jean, 114
radicality, 122–124
real life, intermittency of, 118
reappropriation, patient and, 200
recovery from illness, 101–103
redemption, Christian, and idea of progress, 33–35
Reformation, 16–17
Regelson, William, 57n15
Reich, Wilhelm, 45, 145
reincarnation, 162
relativism, 195
religion: promise of immortality, 126; as source of meaning, 69–70; and vague promises, 33–35
remorse, of modernity, 38
Renaissance, and invention of hell, 15
renunciation: Buddhist doctrine of, 224–226; Christian doctrine of, 9–10
repetition, pleasure of, 74
resentment, and charity, 205
resilience, 209n4

responsibility, 28–29
resurrection of Christ, 20
revisionism, 124
revolt, as response to pain, 203–204, 216
revolutionary movement, and proliferation of suffering, 185
rich, the, 174; Fitzgerald's portrayal of, 168–169; as model of happiness, 163–167
right to die, 59
right to live differently, 140
Rilke, Rainer Maria, 162
Rimbaud, Arthur, 91
Ringley, Jennifer, 76
rollerblading, 91
Romanticism, 138
Romantics, and bourgeoisie, 133–134
Rosset, Clément, 34
Rousseau, Jean-Jacques: on compassion, 204–205; *New Héloïse*, 37
routines, transfiguration of, 74–76. *See also* schedules
Ruysbroek, St. John of, 147

sacraments, Christian, 15
Sade, Marquis de, 45
Saint-Simon (Claude Henri de Rouvroy, comte de Saint-Simon), 28
salvation: as Christian goal, 10–12; and idea of progress, 33–35; and suffering, 20–21; through works or through faith, 12, 16–17
Sartre, Jean-Paul, 77, 136
satisfaction, with present happiness, 114–115

savoir-vivre, rich people as models of, 164
schedules, as constraint, 120–121
Scheler, Max, 20
Schopenhauer, Arthur, 155–156
science, as last adventure, 219
seasonal affective disorder (SAD), 95
Segalen, Victor, 69n1, 148
self-denigration, 143; as bourgeois mode of being, 140–142
self-esteem movement, 50–51
self-fulfillment, as human goal, 43–47
self-hatred, modernity and, 146
self-interest, and bourgeoisie, 133
Seneca, Lucius Annaeus, 170–171
service providers, doctors as, 196
service society, 75
sex, and death, 199
sexuality, and proof of pleasure, 52
Sfez, Lucien, 142n12
sickness. *See* illness
Simonnot, Philippe, 170
sin, arising from prohibitions, 45
situationists, 117, 124–125
skeptic, patient as, 196
Smith, Adam, 28
snowboarding, 91
socialism, and proliferation of suffering, 185
social mobility, 149
Socrates, 186n2
Sollers, Philippe, 157
Solon, 161
Sombart, Werner, 137
Sontag, Susan, 188
Spengler, Oswald, 170
Spinoza, Benedict, 65, 105, 177, 216

spirituality, and pursuit of health, 55–56

spontaneity, 127–128; formalism of, 157–158

sports, 191, 209

Stalin, Joseph, 138

Stancer, Rosie, 210

state of grace, 58

Steiner, George, 81, 208

stock exchange, 175

Stoicism, 194, 218; and *praemeditatio,* 211; and suffering, 21

stress, and everyday life, 79–82

sufferers: coalitions of, 197–200; exemplary, 212–219

suffering: absurdity of, 188; avoidance of, 4–5; as basis of rights, 189–191; in Buddhism, 224–225; in Christianity, 20–26; concealment of, 186–187; as crime, 183–184; denial of reality of, 183–184; distinct from salutary adversity, 207; "good," 206–212; growing aversion to, 33; and human limitations, 223–224; and idea of progress, 31–33; as identity, 101–103; market in, 192–193; meaninglessness of, 36–37; modern impatience with, 220; as mystery, 23; of newborn, 32–33; new culture of, 192–195; as norm, 22–23; outstanding examples of, 212–219; pathology of, 65–66; persistence of, 35–38; power of word, 189; proliferation of, 184–192; and speechlessness, 186–187; and spiritual renewal, 20–21; temporary armistices with, 219–224; of terminal patients, 32–33

superman, Nietzschean, 217

superrich, 174

supreme Good, 5

surfing, 91, 96

surprise, blessed, 147–148, 153

surrealism, and "wonder of the everyday," 118–119

surrealists, 124–125

survivorship, 105

Svevo, Italo, 101–102

syncretism, 226

Talleyrand (Charles Maurice de Talleyrand-Périgord), 133

tardiness, 120–121

Taylor, Charles, 230

teacher, Buddhist, 225

television weather channels, 94

temporality: and everyday life, 76–83; and modernity, 70–74; and monastic life, 84–86; in religious worldview, 69–70

Teresa, Mother, 22

terminal patients, 32–33, 220–224

terrorist attack, response to, 197–200, 202n11

thriller, as genre, 103–104

Tibetan cause, 59–61

Tolstoy, Leo, 186–187; *Death of Ivan Ilyich,* 187n3

totalitarianism, 40–41

trash, propagation of, 184–192

trauma, collective response to, 197–200

triviality, focus on, 87–90

Trouille, Clovis, 158

ultrarich, 174

uncertainty, over suffering and nonsuffering, 191–192

unemployment, 165
unhappiness, 128; as failure to be happy, 5; immorality of, 48–51; over not being happy, 65–66; of the rich, 164
United States: and morality of frugality, 175–177; poverty in, 176n4; and vulgarity, 155–156
utilitarianism, 28, 30–31, 42n2, 143–145
utopia: of fun, 91–92; of permanent happiness, 115–120

Valéry, Paul, 20
Vaneigem, Raoul, 117; *Traité de savoir-vivre...*, 43–45, 139n10
Veblen, Thorstein, 173
Vergely, 208
Verlaine, Paul, 77
victims, power of, 201–202
victim status, competition over, 192–193
Vigny, Alfred de, 161
Villiers de L'Isle-Adam (Jean-Marie-Mathias-Philippe-Auguste, comte de Villiers de l'Isle-Adam), 145
virtual cemeteries, 221
virtual technologies, 92
Voltaire (François-Marie Arouet), 188; *Candide*, 37, 206; *Le Mondain*, 27

vulgarity, 149–151; and imitation, 153–156; and modernity, 156–160

war, 136–142
Warhol, Andy, 159
Watzlawick, Paul, 62
weather, passion for, 92–98
Weber, Max, 143
Weil, Simone, 21
well-being: increased availability of, 165–166; politics of, 143–146
West, Buddhism in, 224–226
West, Paul, 214–216, 218
Western, genre of, 103–104
will, and autonomy, 210
Woolf, Virginia, *Mrs. Dalloway*, 74
World Health Organization, 55, 101
writing, as locus of happiness, 82, 216

Xenophon, 208

Young, Neil, 81
youth: cult of, 54; and death, 199

Zeno, 186n2
"zero casualty" policy, in military, 139
Zola, Émile, 112, 135, 151
Zorn, Fritz, 212–213, 216–217, 217n11